DK EYEWITNESS

MINI MAP+GUIDE
ROME

GW00645162

CONTENTS

EXPERIENCE

Left: Skyline from the Victor Emmanuel
Monument Right: The Spanish Steps

NEED TO KNOW

KEY TO MAIN ICONS

🗺	Map	🚊	Tram
📍	Address/Location	🚌	Bus
📞	Telephone	ℹ	Visitor information
🚆	Train	🕐	Open
Ⓜ	Metro	🚫	Closed
		🌐	Website

**The information in this DK Eyewitness Travel
Guide is checked regularly.**
Every effort has been made to ensure this book is
up-to-date at the time of going to press. However,
details such as addresses, opening hours, prices and
travel information, are liable to change. The
publishers cannot accept responsibility for any
consequences arising from the use of this book, nor
for any material on third-party websites. If you have
any comments, please email: travelguides@dk.com.

Penguin
Random
House

Main Contributors Ros Belford,
Olivia Ercoli, Roberta Mitchell
Design Nidhi Mehra, Priyanka Thakur
Editorial Rachel Fox, Shikha Kulkarni,
Arushi Mathur, Beverly Smart
Indexer Manjari Thakur
Picture Research Sumita Khatwani, Ellen Root
Cartography Suresh Kumar, Casper Morris
Jacket Designers Maxine Pedliham, Amy Cox
DTP Narender Kumar, Jason Little, Tanveer Zaidi
Delhi Team Head Malavika Talukder
Art Director Maxine Pedliham
Publishing Director Georgina Dee
Conceived by Priyanka Thakur
and Shikha Kulkarni

Printed and bound in China

Content previously published in
DK Eyewitness Rome (2019).
This abridged edition first published in 2020

Published in Great Britain by Dorling Kindersley
Limited, DK, One Embassy Gardens, 8 Viaduct
Gardens, London SW11 7BW, UK

The authorised representative in the EEA is
Dorling Kindersley Verlag GmbH. Arnulfstr.
124, 80636 Munich, Germany

Published in the United States by DK Publishing,
1745 Broadway, 20th Floor, New York, NY 10019, USA

23 10 9 8 7 6 5 4 3

A CIP catalogue record is available
from the British Library.

A catalogue record for this book is available
from the Library of Congress.
ISBN 978-0-2413-9778-7

MIX
Paper | Supporting
responsible forestry

FSC™ C018179

This book was made with Forest Stewardship
Council™ certified paper – one small step in
DK's commitment to a sustainable future.
For more information go to
www.dk.com/our-green-pledge

WELCOME TO
ROME

Hugely photogenic, with its spectacular piazzas, cascading fountains and exuberant street life, Rome is a Baroque extravaganza just waiting for you to join in la dolce vita. Linger over a Campari Spritz in a pavement café, marvel at world-famous art, immerse yourself in ancient history and spook yourself in underground catacombs.

Rome brings history to life like no other city. Whether visiting the Colosseum, the temples and basilicas of the Forum, or the Pantheon, you can travel back in time to ancient Rome. At the Baths of Caracalla and Palazzo Valentini digital technology restores ancient ruins to their former glory. For spectacular views over the whole city climb the cupola of St Peter's, then see God create Adam on the world-famous Sistine Chapel ceiling. Immerse yourself in the Baroque euphoria of Piazza Navona, float down the Spanish Steps, throw a coin in the Trevi Fountain, dive into the food markets of Campo de' Fiori and Testaccio and experience the vibrant nightlife of Trastevere and the hipster bars and restaurants of Monti. Rome's large central park, Villa Borghese, provides a peaceful green refuge, where you can also see an extraordinary collection of Bernini sculptures in the Museo Borghese.

It's not surprising that Rome, with a huge number of ancient sites, museums, churches and galleries, can feel a little overwhelming. To help, we've broken the city down into easily navigable chapters, highlighting each area's unmissable sights and unexpected delights. Add insider tips, a comprehensive fold-out map and a need-to-know section full of expert advice for before and during your trip and you've got an indispensable guidebook. Whatever your ideal break includes, this DK Eyewitness Mini Map and Guide to Rome is your perfect travel companion. Enjoy the book and enjoy Rome.

↓ Fontana dei Quattro Fiumi
on Piazza Navona

CAPITOL

This is the monumental heart of ancient and modern Rome. The white marble behemoth of the Victor Emmanuel Monument, the focus of patriotic ceremonies and political demonstrations, dominates heavily trafficked Piazza Venezia. Behind it, Capitol Hill has been the seat of municipal government since ancient times. Civic marriages still take place in the registry office of the Palazzo del Senatore, which, together with the Palazzo dei Conservatori and Palazzo Nuovo housing the Capitoline Museums, frame the elegant Piazza del Campidoglio.

↓ The Capitoline Museums on Piazza del Campidoglio

↑ The frescoed interior of the Palazzo dei Conservatori

CAPITOLINE MUSEUMS

📍 W5 🏛 Piazza del Campidoglio 1 🚌 63, 70, 75, 81, 87, 160, 170, 204, 628, 716 and other routes to Piazza Venezia 🚊 8 🕘 9:30am-7:30pm daily
🌐 museicapitolini.org

This museum of Classical sculpture is housed in two palaces – Palazzo dei Conservatori and Palazzo Nuovo – either side of Piazza del Campidoglio.

The Capitoline collection began in 1471 when Pope Sixtus IV donated several Classical bronze statues from his personal collection, including the She-Wolf, to the city. The She-Wolf was displayed on the façade of the Palazzo dei Conservatori, and rapidly became the symbol of Rome. Located in two majestic palaces, both with façades designed by Michelangelo, the collection has grown over the centuries to become Rome's finest and most famous assemblage of Classical sculpture. Palazzo dei Conservatori also houses a lovely gallery of Renaissance art. In 1734 Pope Clement XII Corsini decreed that the collection be turned into what is considered to be the world's first public museum.

EAT & DRINK

Caffetteria dei Musei Capitolini
The big draw of this café-restaurant on the top floor of the Capitoline Museums is its vast terrace with a panoramic view taking in rooftops and assorted ruins. The vista is especially spectacular at sundown. Opt for superior coffee and cake or an aperitivo and a snack. The café is also open to non-ticket-holders via a separate entrance on Piazzale Caffarelli.

📍 W5 🏛 Piazzale Caffarelli 4
🌐 museicapitolini. org/it/oltre_il_ museo/caffetteria

EXPERIENCE MORE

Roman Insula

📍 W4 🏛 Piazza d'Aracoeli 🚌 40, 62, 63, 64, 110, 170 🚊 8
🚫 To the public

Two thousand years ago the urban poor of Rome used to make their homes in *insulae* – apartment blocks. These were often badly maintained by landlords, and expensive to rent in a city where land costs were high. This 2nd-century AD tenement block, of barrel-vault construction, is the only survivor in Rome from that era. The fourth, fifth and part of the sixth storey remain above current ground level. It is closed to the public but you can view its exterior from the street. In the Middle Ages, a section of the upper storeys was converted into a church; look out for the bell tower and 14th-century Madonna.

During the Fascist years, the area was cleared, and three lower floors emerged. Some 380 people may have lived in the tenement, in the squalid conditions described by the 1st-century AD satirical writers Martial and Juvenal. The latter mentions that he had to climb 200 steps to reach his garret.

This *insula* may once have had more storeys. The higher you lived, the more dismal the conditions, as the poky spaces of the building's upper levels testify.

Santa Maria in Aracoeli

📍 W4 🏛 Piazza d'Aracoeli (entrances via Aracoeli Staircase and door behind Palazzo Nuovo) 📞 06-6976 3839 🚌 40, 62, 63, 64, 110, 170 🚊 8 ⏰ summer: 9am-6:30pm daily; winter: 9am-5:30pm daily

Dating from at least the 6th century, the church of Santa Maria in Aracoeli, or St Mary of the Altar in the Sky, stands on the northern summit of the Capitoline, on the site of the ancient temple to Juno. Its 22 columns were taken from various ancient buildings; the inscription on the third column to the left tells us that it comes *"a cubiculo Augustorum"* – from the bedroom of the emperors.

The church of the Roman senators and people, Santa Maria in Aracoeli has been used to celebrate many triumphs over adversity. Its ceiling, with naval motifs, commemorates the Battle of Lepanto (1571), and was built under Pope Gregory XIII Boncompagni, whose family crest, the dragon, can be seen towards the altar end. Many other Roman families and individuals are honoured by memorials in the church. To the right of the entrance door, the tombstone of archdeacon Giovanni Crivelli, rather than being set into the floor of the church, stands eternally to attention, partly so that

the signature "Donatelli" (by Donatello) can be read at eye-level.

The frescoes in the first chapel on the right, painted by Pinturicchio in the 1480s in the beautifully clear style of the early Renaissance, depict St Bernardino of Siena. On the left wall, the perspective of *The Burial of the Saint* slants to the right, taking into account the position of the viewer just outside the chapel. The church is most famous, however, for an icon with apparently miraculous powers, the Santo Bambino. Its powers are said to include resurrecting the dead, and it is sometimes summoned to the bedsides of the gravely ill. Other than at Christmas when the Christ icon sits in the centre of a crib in the second chapel on the left, it is usually to be found in the sacristy, as is the panel of the *Holy Family* from the workshop of Giulio Romano.

The famed Aracoeli Staircase leading to the church numbers 124 marble steps (122 if you start from the right) and was completed in 1348, some say in thanks for the passing of the Black Death, but probably in view of the Holy Year of 1350.

The 14th-century tribune-turned-tyrant Cola di Rienzo used to harangue the masses from the Aracoeli Staircase; in the 17th century foreigners used to sleep on the steps, until Prince Caffarelli, who lived on the hill, scared them off by rolling barrels filled with stones down them.

Popular belief has it that all those who climb the steps of Santa Maria in Aracoeli on their knees will win the Italian national lottery. From the top there is a good view of Rome, with the domes of Sant'Andrea della Valle and St Peter's slightly to the right.

———————————

Piazza del Campidoglio

🚇 W5 🚌 40, 62, 63, 64, 110, 170 🚋 8

When the Holy Roman Emperor Charles V visited Rome in 1536, Pope Paul III Farnese was so embarrassed by the muddy state of the Capitol that he asked Michelangelo to draw up plans for repaving the piazza, and for renovating the façades of the Palazzo dei Conservatori and Palazzo Senatorio.

Michelangelo proposed adding the Palazzo Nuovo to form a piazza in the shape of a trapezium, embellished with Classical sculptures chosen for their relevance to Rome. Building started in 1546 but progressed so slowly that Michelangelo only lived to oversee the double flight of steps at the entrance of Palazzo Senatorio. The piazza was completed in the 17th century, the design remaining largely faithful to the original. Pilasters two storeys high and balustrades interspersed with statues link the buildings thematically. The piazza faces west towards St Peter's, the Christian equivalent of the Capitol. At its centre stands a replica of a statue of Marcus Aurelius. The original is in the Palazzo dei Conservatori.

———————————

Cordonata

🚇 W5 🚌 40, 62, 63, 64, 110, 170 🚋 8

From Piazza Venezia, the Capitol is approached by a gently rising, subtly widening ramp – the Cordonata. At the foot is a pair of granite Egyptian lions, and on the left a 19th-century monument to Cola di Rienzo, close to where the dashing 14th-century tyrant was executed. The top of the ramp is guarded by Classical statues of the Dioscuri – Castor and Pollux.

←

The top of the marble Aracoeli Staircase, with a view across the city

Tarpeian Rock

❼ W5 **⌂ Via di Monte Caprino and Via al Tempio di Giove**
🚌 40, 62, 63, 64, 110, 170 🚎 8

The steep cliff on the southern tip of the Capitoline is called the Tarpeian Rock (*Rupe Tarpea*), after Tarpeia, the young daughter of Spurius Tarpeius, defender of the Capitol in the 8th-century BC Sabine War.

The Sabines, bent on vengeance for the rape of their women by Romulus and his men, bribed Tarpeia to let them up on to the Capitol. As the Augustan historian Livy records, the Sabines used to wear heavy gold bracelets and jewelled rings on their left hands, and Tarpeia's reward for her treachery was to be given "what they wore on their shield-arms".

The Sabines kept to the letter of the bargain if not to its spirit – they repaid Tarpeia not with their jewellery but by crushing her to death between their shields. Tarpeia was possibly the only casualty of her act of treachery – as the invading warriors met the Roman defenders, the Sabine women leapt between the two opposing armies, forcing a reconciliation. The site was subsequently used as a place of execution: traitors and other condemned criminals were thrown over the sheer face of the rock.

Palazzo Venezia and Museum

❼ V4 **⌂ Via del Plebiscito 118** **☎ 06-6999 4388** 🚌 40, 62, 63, 64, 110, 170 **🕐 8:30am-7:30pm Tue-Sun (last adm: 1 hr before closing)**
🚫 1 Jan, 1 May, 25 Dec

The arched windows and doors of this Renaissance civic building are so harmonious that the façade was once attributed to the great Humanist architect Leon Battista Alberti (1404–72). It was more probably built by Giuliano da Maiano, who is known to have carved the fine doorway on to the piazza.

Palazzo Venezia was built in 1455–64 for the Venetian cardinal Pietro Barbo, who later became Pope Paul II. It was at times a papal residence, but it also served as the Venetian Embassy to Rome before passing into French hands in 1797. Since 1916 it has belonged to the state; in the Fascist era, Mussolini used Palazzo Venezia as his headquarters and addressed crowds from the central balcony.

The interior is best seen by visiting the Museo del Palazzo Venezia, Rome's most under-rated museum.

It holds first-class collections of early Renaissance painting; painted wood sculptures and Renaissance chests from Italy; tapestries from all over Europe; majolica; silver; Neapolitan ceramic figurines; Renaissance bronzes; arms and armour; Baroque terracotta sculptures by Bernini, Algardi and others; and 17th- and 18th-century Italian painting. There is a marble screen from the Aracoeli convent, destroyed to make way for the Victor Emmanuel Monument, and a bust of Paul II, showing him to rank with Martin V and Leo X among the fattest-ever popes. The building also hosts major temporary exhibitions.

Temple of Jupiter

❼ W5 **⌂ Via al Tempio di Giove** 🚌 40, 62, 63, 64, 110, 170 **🕐 9:30am-7:30pm daily**

The Temple of Jupiter, the most important in ancient Rome, was founded in honour of the arch-god around 509 BC on the southern summit of the Capitoline Hill. From the few traces that remain, archaeologists have been able to reconstruct the rectangular, Greek appearance of the temple as it once stood. In places it is possible to see remnants of its particularly Roman feature, the podium. Most of this lies

→

The Immaculate Conception by Pier Francesco Mola (1612-66) in the San Marco basilica

beneath the Museo Nuovo wing of the Palazzo dei Conservatori.

By walking around the site, from the podium's southwestern corner in Via del Tempio di Giove to its southeastern corner in Piazzale Caffarelli, you can see that the temple was about the same size as the Pantheon.

San Marco

📍W4 🏛Piazza San Marco 48 📞06-679 5205 🚌40, 62, 63, 64, 110, 170 🚋8 🕐10am-1pm & 4-6pm Tue-Sun (Sat & Sun: to 8pm)

The basilica of San Marco was founded in 336 by Pope Mark, in honour of St Mark the Evangelist. The Pope's relics lie under the altar. The church was restored by Pope Gregory IV in the 9th century.

Further major rebuilding took place in 1455–71, when Pope Paul II Barbo made San Marco the church of the Venetian community in Rome. The blue and gold coffered ceiling is decorated with Pope Paul's heraldic crest, the lion rampant, recalling the lion of St Mark. The appearance of the rest of the interior, with its colonnades of Sicilian jasper, was largely the creation of Filippo Barigioni in the 1740s.

Victor Emmanuel Monument

📍W4 🏛Piazza Venezia 📞06-678 3587 🚌40, 62, 63, 64, 110, 170 🚋8 🕐Summer: 9:30am-5:30pm daily; winter: 9:30am-4:30pm daily (last adm: 30 mins before closing)

Known as Il Vittoriano, this monument was begun in 1885 and inaugurated in 1911 in honour of Victor Emmanuel II of Savoy, the first king of a unified Italy. The king is depicted here in a gilt bronze equestrian statue, oversized like the monument itself – the statue is 12 m (39 ft) long.

The edifice also contains a museum of the Risorgimento, the events that led to unification. Built in white Brescian marble, the "wedding cake" (just one of its many nicknames) can be seen from almost every part of Rome and will never mellow into the ochre tones of surrounding buildings. It is widely held to be the epitome of self-important, insensitive architecture, though the views it offers are spectacular. A glass lift at the back of the building takes visitors to the very top.

FORUM AND PALATINE

Mussolini's Via dei Fori Imperiali slices above the ruins of the temples and basilicas that once formed the centre of political, commercial and judicial life in ancient Rome. By day it is peppered with souvenir stands and filled with crocodiles of tourists following umbrella-toting guides around the Roman Forum and Colosseum. Some of the Forum ruins are illuminated at night after the tour groups have left and can be viewed from Via dei Fori Imperiali. Crowds are easier to avoid at all times in the green, pine-shaded expanses of the Palatine Hill.

The Colosseum at sunrise ↓

 INSIDER TIP
Roma Pass

Holders of a Roma Pass (p337) and those with timed tickets purchased in advance online gain preferential access. The quietest times to visit are 30 minutes before the scheduled opening time early in the morning or shortly before closing.

Temple of Saturn *(right)* and the Temple of Castor and Pollux *(left)*

THE ROMAN FORUM

📍J6 🏛 Via della Salara Vecchia 5/6 📞 06-3996 7700 🚌 85, 87, 117, 175, 186, 810
🚋3 Ⓜ Colosseo 🕐 8:30am–1 hour before sunset. Admission includes entry to the Colosseum and the Palatine. Tickets can be bought in advance at www.coopculture.it

The Roman Forum was the scene of public meetings, law courts and gladiatorial combats and was lined with shops and open-air markets. It was also the site of many of the city's key temples and monuments.

In the early days of the Republic, the Forum was like a large piazza – a hive of social activity – containing shops, food stalls, temples and the Senate House. By the 2nd century BC it was decided that Rome required a more salubrious centre, and the food stalls were replaced by business centres and law courts. The Forum remained the ceremonial centre of the city under the Empire. Emperors repeatedly renovated old buildings and erected new temples and monuments. To appreciate the layout of the Forum before visiting its confusing patchwork of ruined temples and basilicas, it is best to view the whole area from above, from the Piazza del Campidoglio. Excavation of the Forum continues, and the ruins uncovered date from many different periods of Roman history.

COLOSSEUM

📍K7 🏛Piazza del Colosseo 1 📞06-3996 7700 🚌75, 81, 85, 87, 117, 673, 810
🚋3 to Piazza del Colosseo Ⓜ Colosseo 🕒8:30am–approx 1 hour before sunset daily (last admission 1 hour before closing). Admission includes Palatine and Forum (additional fees for upper tier and guided tours of underground areas). Tickets can be bought in advance at www.coopculture.it

Rome's greatest amphitheatre was commissioned by Emperor Vespasian in AD 72. This magnificent structure was where the Imperial passion for bloody spectacle reached its peak of excess.

Built by Jewish slaves on the marshy site of a lake in the grounds of Nero's palace, the Domus Aurea, the Colosseum was the arena where deadly gladiatorial combats and wild animal fights were staged by the emperor and wealthy citizens for public viewing, free of charge. The Colosseum was built to a practical design, with its 80 arched entrances allowing easy access to 55,000 spectators, but it is also a building of great beauty. It was one of several similar amphitheatres built in the Roman Empire – other surviving examples are at El Djem in North Africa, Nîmes and Arles in France, and Verona in northern

Italy. Despite being damaged over the years by neglect and theft, the Roman Colosseum remains a majestic sight.

The velarium was a huge awning which shaded spectators from the sun.

↑ Inside view of the Colosseum showing remains of the underground rooms where animals were kept

The outer walls are made of travertine. Stone plundered from the façade during the Renaissance was used to build several palaces, bridges and parts of St Peter's.

The vomitorium was the exit used from each numbered section.

Arched entrances (80 in total) were numbered to speed up the entry of the vast crowds.

How Fights were Staged in the Arena

The emperors held shows here, which often began with animals performing circus tricks. Then on came the gladiators, who fought each other to the death. When one was killed, attendants dressed as Charon, the mythical ferryman of the dead, carried his body off on a stretcher, and sand was raked over the blood ready for the next bout. A badly wounded gladiator would surrender his fate to the crowd. Legend has it that the "thumbs up" sign from the emperor meant he could live, "thumbs down" that he die. The victor became a hero. Roman gladiators were usually slaves, prisoners of war or condemned criminals. Most were men, but there were a few female gladiators.

Animals were brought here from as far away as North Africa and the Middle East. The games held in AD 248 to mark the 1,000th anniversary of Rome's founding saw the death of a host of lions, elephants, hippos, zebras and elks in wild-animal hunting spectacles.

A complex of rooms, passages and lifts over several floors lies underneath the arena. Metal fencing kept animals penned in, while archers stood by just in case any escaped. A winch brought the animal cages up to arena level when they were due to fight. A ramp and trap door enabled the animal to reach the arena.

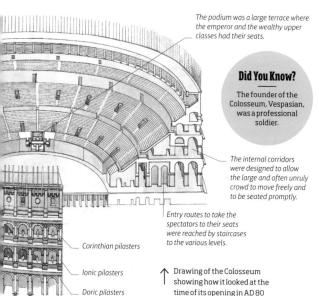

The podium was a large terrace where the emperor and the wealthy upper classes had their seats.

Did You Know?

The founder of the Colosseum, Vespasian, was a professional soldier.

The internal corridors were designed to allow the large and often unruly crowd to move freely and to be seated promptly.

Entry routes to take the spectators to their seats were reached by staircases to the various levels.

Corinthian pilasters

Ionic pilasters

Doric pilasters

↑ Drawing of the Colosseum showing how it looked at the time of its opening in AD 80

The red-brick Trajan's Markets complex, the world's first shopping mall ↑

TRAJAN'S MARKETS

♦ J6 ⌂ Via IV Novembre 94 ☎ 06-0608 🚍 64, 70, 170 and routes to Piazza Venezia ⏰ 9:30am–7:30pm daily (last admission 1 hour before closing)

Originally considered among the wonders of the Classical world, this visionary complex of 150 shops and offices was built by Emperor Trajan and architect Apollodorus of Damascus in the 2nd century AD.

The ancient Roman equivalent of the modern shopping mall, Trajan's Markets is a complex of shops on five levels, selling everything from silks and spices imported from the Middle East to fresh fish, fruit, flowers, wine, oil and fabrics. The top tier was occupied by welfare offices that administered the free corn ration to Roman men and boys. Via Biberatica, the main street, is named after the drinking inns that once lined it. The Torre delle Milizie, the large tower above the Markets, was built in the Middle Ages. The Museo dei Fori Imperiali charts the growth of the extensions to the Roman Forum from Julius Caesar onwards.

EAT

Terre e Domus della Provincia di Roma
Right by Trajan's Markets, this small modern restaurant serves Roman cuisine made with the freshest local ingredients. The *cacio e pepe* (cheese and pepper) pasta is especially good, and there's a very strong wine list.

♦ H5 ⌂ Foro Traiano 82 🌐 palazzo valentini.it/terre-domus

PALATINE

📍 J7 🏠 Via di San Gregorio 30 📞 06-3996 7700 🚌 75, 80, 81, 175, 673, 850
🚋 3 Ⓜ Colosseo 🕐 8:30am–1 hour before sunset. Admission includes entry
to the Forum, Colosseum and Palatine Museum. Tickets can be bought in
advance at www.coopculture.it

The Palatine, once the residence of emperors and aristocrats, is the most pleasant
of Rome's ancient sites. The ruins range from the simple house in which Augustus
is thought to have lived, to the Domus Flavia and Domus Augustana, the public
and private wings of a luxurious palace built by Domitian.

The remains of elaborate fountains, colourful marble floors, fine stone carvings, columns, stuccoes and frescoes can be seen within the magnificent walls of the Imperial palaces. The Palatine Hill is a green haven, shaded by pines, with wild flowers growing among the ancient ruins.

The hill offers fantastic views of the Roman Forum, the Colosseum, the Capitoline Hill and the Circus Maximus. In the 16th century the first private botanical gardens in Europe were built by the Farnese family on the Palatine – the area was dug up during excavations and re-landscaped.

↑ The twins Romulus and Remus, brought up on the Palatine by a wolf, as per legend

← The Palatine Hill viewed through an arch of the neighbouring Colosseum

EXPERIENCE MORE

Trajan's Column

📍 H6 🏛 Via dei Fori Imperiali 🚌 64, 70, 170 and routes to Piazza Venezia

This elegant marble column was inaugurated by Trajan in AD 113, and celebrates his two campaigns in Dacia (Romania) in AD 101–3 and AD 107–8. The column, base and pedestal are 40 m (131 ft) tall – precisely the same height as the spur of Quirinal Hill excavated to make room for Trajan's Forum.

Spiralling up the column are minutely detailed scenes from the campaigns. The column is pierced with small windows to illuminate its internal spiral staircase (closed to the public).

When Trajan died in AD 117 his ashes were placed in a golden urn in the hollow base of the column. The column's survival was largely due to the intervention of Pope Gregory the Great (reigned 590–604). He was so moved by a relief of Trajan helping a woman whose son had

← Trajan's Column topped with a statue of St Peter

been killed that he begged God to release the emperor's soul from hell. God duly appeared to the pope to say that Trajan had been rescued, but asked him not to pray for the souls of any more pagans.

Legend has it that when Trajan's ashes were exhumed his skull and tongue were not only intact, but his tongue told of his release from hell. The land around the column was then declared sacred and the column was spared. In 1587, the statue of Trajan atop the column was replaced with one of St Peter.

Palazzo Valentini

📍 H5 🏛 Via IV Novembre 119/a 🕘 9:30am-6:30pm Wed-Mon; visits by guided tour only 🌐 palazzo valentini.it

During maintenance work in the basement of Palazzo Valentini in 2005, the remains of two houses belonging to a leading patrician family of Imperial ancient Rome were discovered. Elegant living rooms, courtyards, a kitchen and a private baths complex were revealed, complete with traces of their elaborate original decorations – mosaics, frescoes and coloured marbles.

GREAT VIEW
Trajan's Column

At Palazzo Valentini there are screenings of a brilliant animation of the bas-reliefs of Trajan's Column. Be sure to book in advance.

Using digital technology, light and sound effects, film and projections, the houses have been "reconstructed", creating a virtual-reality museum. There are tours in English and Italian.

Forum of Caesar

📍 H6 🏛 Via del Carcere Tulliano 📞 06-0608 🚌 85, 87, 186, 810, 850 🕘 By appt only

The first of Rome's Imperial fora was built by Julius Caesar. He spent a fortune buying up and demolishing houses on the site. Pride of place went to a temple dedicated in 46 BC to the goddess Venus Genetrix, from whom Caesar claimed descent. The temple contained statues of Caesar and Cleopatra as well as of Venus. All that remains is a platform and three Corinthian columns. The forum was enclosed by a double colonnade sheltering a row of shops, but this burned down in AD 80 and was rebuilt by Domitian and Trajan.

→ The remains of the Forum of Caesar, the first of Rome's Imperial fora

Some parts are visible from above in Via dei Fori Imperiali.

Mamertine Prison

Q H6 **⌂** Clivo Argentario 1 **C** 06-698 961 **🚌** 85, 87, 186, 810 **🕐** 8:30am-4:30pm daily (guided tours by appt only; call for details)

Below the 16th-century church of San Giuseppe dei Falegnami (St Joseph of the Carpenters) is a dank dungeon in which, according to Christian legend, St Peter was imprisoned. He is said to have caused a spring to bubble up into the cell, using the water to baptize his guards.

The prison was in an old cistern with access to the city's main sewer (the Cloaca Maxima). The lower cell was used for executions and bodies were thrown into the sewer. The Gaulish leader Vercingetorix, defeated by Julius Caesar in 52 BC, was executed here.

Arch of Constantine

Q J7 **⌂** Between Via di San Gregorio and Piazza del Colosseo **🚌** 75, 85, 87, 673, 810 **🚋** 3 **M** Colosseo

This arch was dedicated in AD 315 to mark Constantine's victory three years before over his co-emperor, Maxentius. Constantine claimed he owed his victory to a vision of Christ, but there is nothing Christian about the arch – most of the medallions, reliefs and statues were scavenged from earlier monuments. Inside the arch are reliefs of Trajan's victory over the Dacians, probably by the same artist who worked on Trajan's Column.

Forum of Nerva

Q J6 **⌂** Piazza del Grillo 1 (via the Forum of Augustus) **C** 06-0608 **🚌** 85, 87, 186, 810 **⟲** To the public but viewable from above

The Forum of Nerva was begun by his predecessor, Domitian, and completed in AD 97. Little more than a long corridor with a colonnade along the sides and a Temple of Minerva at one end, it was also known as the Forum Transitorium because it lay between the Forum of Peace, built by Vespasian in AD 70, and the Forum of Augustus. Vespasian's forum is almost completely covered by Via dei Fori Imperiali, as is much of the Forum of Nerva. Excavations have unearthed shops and taverns, but only part of the forum can be seen.

PIAZZA DELLA ROTONDA

The compact core of cobbled streets and piazza around the Pantheon is crammed with churches and palaces, restaurants, cafés and enticing gelaterias. Businessmen remonstrate into their phones, chauffeurs leap into action as paparazzi pounce on politicians, ice-cream eaters and tourists jam the streets. Hidden in the back streets are fragments from a temple of Isis, shops selling ecclesiastical paraphernalia and the ancient Temple of Hadrian, while the church of Sant'Ignazio di Loyola holds magnificent *trompe l'oeil* frescoes.

Piazza della Rotonda, bordered by the Pantheon and lively cafés ↓

The splendid, highly ornate main nave and altar inside the Gesù

GESÙ

⬤ V4 ⬤ Piazza del Gesù ⬤ 06-697 001 ⬤ H, 46, 62, 64, 70, 81, 87, 186, 492, 628, 810 and other routes ⬤ 8 ⬤ 7am-12:30pm & 4-7:45pm daily

Dating from between 1568 and 1584, the Gesù was the first Jesuit church to be built in Rome. Its design has been much imitated throughout the Catholic world.

Epitomizing Counter-Reformation and Baroque architecture, the layout proclaims the church's two major functions: a large nave with side pulpits for preaching to crowds, and a main altar as the centrepiece for the celebration of the Mass. By providing people with prayer books and filling the nave with enough light for people to read, the Jesuits hoped to increase the popularity of Catholicism during the Thirty Years' War when Catholics were losing followers to the Protestants. The illusionistic decoration by Il Baciccia in the nave and dome was added after the war in the late 17th century. Its message is clear and triumphant: faithful Catholic worshippers will be joyfully uplifted into the heavens while Protestants and other heretics are flung into hell's fires.

ST IGNATIUS AND THE JESUIT ORDER

Spanish soldier Ignatius of Loyola (1491-1556) joined the Church after being wounded in battle in 1521. He came to Rome in 1537 and founded the Jesuits, sending missionaries and teachers all over the world to win souls for Catholicism.

PANTHEON

📍U3 🏛Piazza della Rotonda 🚌116 and routes along Via del Corso, Corso Vittorio Emanuele II and Corso del Rinascimento 🕐9am-7:30pm Mon-Sat, 9am-6pm Sun, 9am-1pm public hols 🌐pantheonroma.com

With its awe-inspiring domed interior, the Pantheon – the Roman temple of "all the gods" – is the best-preserved ancient building in Rome. Unlike many other Roman structures that fell into disrepair, it became a church in the 7th century, ensuring its continued use and conservation.

The interior of the church is dominated by the vast hemispherical dome, which has both a height and diameter of 43.3 m (142 ft). The hole at the top of the dome, the oculus, provides the only light; we owe this marvel of engineering to the Emperor Hadrian, who designed the structure (AD 118–125) to replace an earlier temple built by Marcus Agrippa, son-in-law of Augustus. The shrines that line the wall of the Pantheon range from the Tomb of Raphael to those of the kings of Italy.

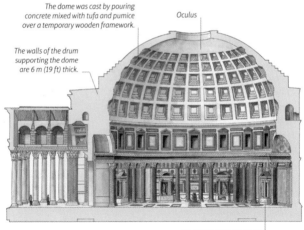

The dome was cast by pouring concrete mixed with tufa and pumice over a temporary wooden framework.

Oculus

The walls of the drum supporting the dome are 6 m (19 ft) thick.

The Tomb of Raphael rests below a Madonna sculpture by Lorenzetto (1520).

↑ Illustration of the Pantheon

EXPERIENCE MORE

Fontanella del Facchino

📍V3 🚇Via Lata 🚌64, 81, 85, 117, 119, 492 and many other routes

Il Facchino (the Porter), once in the Corso, now set in the wall of the Banco di Roma, was one of Rome's "talking statues" like Pasquino. Created around 1590, the fountain may have been based on a drawing by painter Jacopino del Conte. The statue of a man holding a barrel most likely represents a member of the Università degli Acquaroli (Fraternity of Water-carriers), though it is also said to be of Martin Luther, or of the porter Abbondio Rizzio, who died carrying a barrel.

Piazza di Sant'Ignazio

📍V2 & 3 🚌117, 119, 492 and routes along Via del Corso or stopping at Piazza San Silvestro

One of the major works of the Roman Rococo, Piazza di Sant'Ignazio (1727–8) is Filippo Raguzzini's masterpiece. It offsets the imposing façade of the church of Sant'Ignazio with the intimacy of the houses belonging to the bourgeoisie. The theatrical setting, the curvilinear design and the playful forms of its windows, balconies and balusters mark the piazza as one of a highly distinct group of structures. Along with Palazzo Doria Pamphilj (1731), the façade of La Maddalena (1735) and the aristocratic Spanish Steps (1723), it belongs to the moment when Rome's opulent Rococo triumphed over conservative Classicism.

San Lorenzo in Lucina

📍V1 🚇Via in Lucina 16A 📞06-6871494 🚌81, 117, 492, 628 🕐8am-8pm daily

The church is one of Rome's oldest Christian places of worship, and was probably built on a well sacred to Juno, protectress of women. It was rebuilt during the 12th century, and today's external appearance is quite typical of the period, featuring a portico with reused Roman columns crowned by medieval capitals, a plain triangular pediment and a Romanesque bell tower with coloured marble inlay.

The interior was totally rebuilt in 1856–8. The old basilica plan was destroyed and the two side naves were replaced by Baroque chapels. Do not miss the fine bust in the Fonseca Chapel, designed by Bernini, or the *Crucifixion* by Guido Reni above the main altar. There is also a 19th-century monument honouring French painter Nicolas Poussin, who died in Rome in 1655 and was buried in the church.

La Maddalena

📍U2 🏛Piazza della Maddalena 📞06-899 281 🚌116 and many routes along Via del Corso and Corso Vittorio Emanuele II ⏰8:30-11:30am & 5-6:30pm daily (9-11:30am Sat)

Situated in a small piazza near the Pantheon, the Maddalena, built in 1735, has a Rococo façade that epitomizes the love of light and movement of the late Baroque. Its curves are reminiscent of Borromini's San Carlo alle Quattro Fontane. The façade has been lovingly restored, although die-hard Neo-Classicists dismiss its painted stucco as icing sugar. The small size of the Maddalena did not deter the 17th- and 18th-century decorators who filled the interior with ornaments from the floor to the top of the elegant cupola. The organ loft and choir are particularly powerful examples of the Baroque's desire to fire the imagination of the faithful. Many of the paintings and sculptures found within the Maddalena adopt the Christian imagery of the Counter-Reformation. In the niches of the nave, the statues are personifications of virtues such as Humility and Simplicity. There are also scenes from the life of St Camillus de Lellis, who died in the adjacent convent in 1614. The church belonged to his followers, the Camillians, a preaching order active in Rome's hospitals. Like the Jesuits, they commissioned powerful works of art to convey the force of their religious message.

Palazzo di Montecitorio

📍V2 🏛Piazza di Monte Citorio 🚌116 and all routes along Via del Corso or stopping at Piazza San Silvestro ⏰Usually 1st Sun each month (except Jul & Aug); ticket office opens 9:30am, with first guided visit 10:30am & last entry 3:30pm 🌐camera.it

The palazzo's first architect, Bernini, was appointed after he presented a silver model of his design to the wife of his patron, Prince Ludovisi. The building was completed in 1694 by Carlo Fontana and became the Papal Tribunal of Justice. In 1871 it was chosen to be Italy's new Chamber of Deputies, and by 1927 it had doubled in size, with a second grand façade. The 630 members of the Italian parlia-ment are elected by a majority system with proportional representation. Guided tours take place in the plenary hall and reception rooms.

Santa Maria sopra Minerva

📍V3 🏛Piazza della Minerva 42 📞06-679 3926 🚌116 and routes along Via del Corso, Via del Plebiscito and Corso Vittorio Emanuele II ⏰10:30am-12:30pm & 3-7pm daily

Few other churches display such a complete and impressive record of Italian art. Dating from the 13th century, the Minerva is one of the few examples of Gothic architecture in Rome. It was the traditional stronghold of

the Dominicans, whose anti-heretical zeal earned them the nickname of *Domini Canes* (hounds of the Lord).

Built on ancient ruins, supposed to have been the Temple of Minerva, the simple T-shaped vaulted building acquired rich chapels and works of art by which its many patrons wished to be remembered. Note the Cosmatesque 13th-century tombs and the exquisite works of 15th-century Tuscan and Venetian artists. Local talent of the period can be admired in Antoniazzo Romano's *Annunciation*, featuring Cardinal Juan de Torquemada, uncle of the infamous Spanish Inquisitor.

The more monumental style of the Roman Renaissance can be seen in the tombs of the 16th-century Medici popes, Leo X and his cousin Clement VII, and

The façade of Palazzo Montecitorio, the Italian Chamber of Deputies

in the richly decorated Aldobrandini Chapel. Near the steps of the choir is the celebrated sculpture of the *Risen Christ*, started by Michelangelo but completed by Raffaello da Montelupo in 1521. There are also splendid works of art from the Baroque period, including a tomb and a bust by Bernini.

The church also contains the tombs of many famous Italians: St Catherine of Siena, who died here in 1380; the Venetian sculptor Andrea Bregno (died 1506); the Humanist Cardinal Pietro Bembo (died 1547); and Fra Angelico, the Dominican friar and painter, who died in Rome in 1455.

Originally meant to decorate Palazzo Barberini as a joke, the elephant and obelisk sculpture in front of the church is typical of Bernini's inexhaustible imagination. (The elephant was actually sculpted by Ercole Ferrata to Bernini's design.) When the ancient obelisk was found in the garden of the monastery of Santa Maria sopra Minerva, the friars wanted the monument erected in their piazza. Despite opposition from Bernini, the elephant was provided with a cube underneath it (partly covered by an enormous saddle-cloth) at the insistance of a friar, who was Bernini's rival. The friar claimed that the gap under

the animal's abdomen would undermine its stability. Bernini knew better, however: you need only look at the Fontana dei Quattro Fiumi in Piazza Navona to appreciate his use of empty space.

Temple of Hadrian

📍 V2 🏛 La Borsa, Piazza di Pietra 🚌 117, 119, 492 and routes along Via del Corso or stopping at Piazza San Silvestro ⏰ For exhibitions

This temple honours the Emperor Hadrian as a god and was dedicated by his son and successor, Antoninus Pius in AD 145. The remains of the temple are visible on the southern side of Piazza di Pietra, incorporated in a 17th-century building. This was originally a papal customs house, completed by Carlo Fontana and his son in the 1690s. Today the building houses the Roman stock exchange (La Borsa).

Eleven marble Corinthian columns 15 m (49 ft) high stand on a base of *peperino*, a volcanic rock quarried from the Alban hills, to the south of Rome. The columns decorated the northern flank of the temple enclosing its inner shrine, the *cella*. The *peperino* wall of the *cella* is still visible behind the columns, as is part of the coffered portico ceiling.

PIAZZA NAVONA

An exuberantly Baroque oval dominated by the towering obelisk and cascading waters of Bernini's Fontana dei Quattro Fiumi, Piazza Navona is the social heart of Rome. An outdoor salon fringed with pricey pavement cafés, it is full from morning to night with tourists, Romans, buskers, mime-artists and itinerant street vendors. The picturesque cobbled streets around it are home to places to sleep, eat and drink that run the gamut from super-chic to super-cheap. Antiques shops, vintage clothes stores and some extremely stylish fashion, shoe and design boutiques are found here too.

↓ Street artists in Piazza Navona

↑ Piazza Navona, with the Fontana del Moro in the foreground

PIAZZA NAVONA

📍 T2 🚌 46, 62, 64, 70, 81, 87, 116, 492, 628

No other piazza in Rome can rival the theatricality of Piazza Navona. The social centre of the city, the piazza buzzes with life day and night.

Rome's most famous and theatrical piazza is surrounded by cafés and dominated by the Egyptian obelisk, cascading waters and gleaming marble statues of Bernini's Fontana dei Quattro Fiumi. Located on the site of an ancient Roman stadium, the oval piazza has long been a lively part of Rome. In the Renaissance years there was a market here. Today the square is equally bustling, and is especially spectacular at night when the fountains are flood-lit and the café-terraces illuminated with flame-throwing lamps.

Fountains

Work on Bernini's Fontana dei Quattro Fiumi in the centre of the square started in 1648, and was financed by a tax levied on bread, even though there was a famine at the time. The fountain is thought to symbolize the power of the papacy over the entire world,

represented by the four rivers (Plate, Ganges, Nile and Danube). The obelisk originally stood on the Appian Way, and sits on a sculpted rock, decorated with the dove and olive branch emblems from Pope Innocent X's coat of arms. Featuring a Moor wrestling with a dolphin, the Fontana del Moro at the southern end was originally designed by Giacomo della Porta and consisted simply of the dolphin and four Tritons. In 1653, Bernini embellished it by designing the statue of a Moor to straddle the dolphin. In 1874, the original was moved to the Galleria Borghese and replaced with a copy.

At the northern end of the square, the Fontana del Nettuno began as a public drinking and washing fountain, with a basin designed by Giacomo della Porta. In the late 19th century Romans no longer depended on public fountains for their water supplies, and the fountain became a purely decorative one.

EAT

Tre Scalini
This terrace café is famous for its *tartufo* - dense dark chocolate ice cream made from 13 varieties of Swiss chocolate studded with shards of bitter chocolate and served with a wafer and smear of whipped cream.

📍 T2 🏠 Piazza Navona 28
☎ 06-6880 1996

EXPERIENCE MORE

Santa Maria della Pace

📍 T2 🏛 Vicolo dell'Arco della Pace 5 🚌 46, 62, 64, 70, 81, 87, 116, 492, 628
🕐 9:30am–6:30pm daily

A drunken soldier allegedly pierced the breast of a painted Madonna on this site, causing it to bleed. Pope Sixtus IV della Rovere (reigned 1471–84) placated the Virgin by ordering Baccio Pontelli to build her a church if she would bring the war with Turkey to an end. Peace was restored and the church was named Santa Maria della Pace (St Mary of Peace).

The cloister was added by Bramante in 1504. As in his famous round chapel, the Tempietto (p275), he scrupulously followed

Classical rules of proportion and achieved a monumental effect in a relatively small space. Pietro da Cortona may have had Bramante's Tempietto in mind when he added the church's charming semicircular portico in 1656. The interior, a short nave ending under an octagonal cupola, houses Raphael's famous frescoes of four *Sibyls*, and four *Prophets* by his pupil Timoteo Viti, painted for the banker Agostino Chigi in 1514. Baldassarre Peruzzi also did some work in the church (he painted the fresco in the first chapel on the left), as did the architect Antonio da Sangallo the Younger, who designed the second chapel on the right.

Sant'Agostino

📍 U2 🏛 Piazza di Sant' Agostino 80 🚌 70, 81, 87, 116, 186, 492, 628 🕐 7:30am–noon & 4–7:30pm daily

One of the earliest of Rome's Renaissance

←

Detail of Raphael's fresco depicting four Sibyls (c.1514), in the Chigi Chapel of Santa Maria della Pace

churches – and with a façade made of travertine taken from the Colosseum – Sant'Agostino is associated with mothers, thanks to a statue of the Madonna del Parto (Pregnant Madonna) by Jacopo Sansovino that is believed to have the power to help pregnant women. The Virgin's Classical features and heavy drapery suggest she may have been inspired by a statue of Juno Lucina, the Roman goddess of childbirth. Don't miss the extraordinary Madonna di Loreto by Caravaggio. Depicting a peasant-like Madonna standing in a doorway welcoming two pilgrims, it is remarkably – and, at the time, controversially – realistic. The soles of the pilgrims' feet are filthy, and even the Madonna has dirty toenails.

Palazzo Madama

📍 U3 🏛 Corso del Rinascimento 🚌 70, 81, 87, 116, 186, 492, 628 🕐 10am–6pm generally first Sat of month (excluding Aug); tickets available from 8:30am on day of visit 🌐 senato.it

This 16th-century palazzo was built for the Medici family. It was the residence of Medici cousins Giovanni and Giuliano, both of whom became popes: Giovanni as Leo X and Giuliano as

←

The Baroque decoration on the ceiling and columns inside the church of San Luigi dei Francesi

Angel. The first version of this last painting was rejected because of its vivid realism; never before had a saint been shown as a tired old man with dirty feet. All three Caravaggios in San Luigi dei Francesi display very disquieting realism and a highly dramatic use of light.

Clement VII. Caterina de' Medici, Clement VII's niece, also lived here before she was married to Henri, son of King François I of France, in 1533.

The palazzo takes its name from Madama Margherita of Austria, illegitimate daughter of Emperor Charles V, who married Alessandro de' Medici and, after his death, Ottavio Farnese. Thus, part of the art collection of the Florentine Medici family was inherited by the Roman Farnese family.

The spectacular façade was built in the mid-17th century by Cigoli and Paolo Maruccelli. The latter gave it an ornate cornice and whimsical decorative details on the roof. Since 1871 the palazzo has been the seat of the upper house of the Italian parliament.

San Luigi dei Francesi

📍 U2 🏛 Piazza di San Luigi dei Francesi 5 📞 06-688 271 🚌 70, 81, 87, 116, 186, 492, 628 🕐 9:30am–12:45pm & 2:30–6:30pm daily (Sat: to 12:15pm & 6pm; Sun: from 11:30am)

The French national church was founded in 1518, but it took until 1589 to complete. It holds the tombs of many illustrious French people, including Chateaubriand's lover Pauline de Beaumont, who died in Rome in 1805.

Three Caravaggio masterpieces hang in the fifth chapel on the left, all dedicated to St Matthew. Painted between 1597 and 1602, these were Caravaggio's first great religious works: the *Calling of St Matthew*, the *Martyrdom of St Matthew* and *St Matthew and the*

Palazzo Pamphilj

📍 T3 🏛 Piazza Navona 14 🚌 46, 62, 64, 70, 81, 87, 116, 492, 628 🔓 For guided tours only 🌐 roma.itamaraty.gov.br

In 1644 Giovanni Battista Pamphilj became Pope Innocent X. During his ten-year reign, he heaped riches on his own family, especially his domineering sister-in-law, Olimpia Maidalchini. The "talking statue" Pasquino gave her the nickname "Olim-Pia", Latin for "formerly virtuous". She lived in the grand Palazzo Pamphilj, which has wonderful 17th-century frescoes by Pietro da Cortona depicting scenes from the life of Aeneas and a gallery by Borromini. The building now houses the Brazilian embassy and cultural centre.

Palazzo Massimo alle Colonne

⚲ T3 ⌂ Corso Vittorio Emanuele II 141 ▦ 40, 46, 62, 64, 70, 81, 87, 116, 186, 492, 628

During the last two years of his life, Baldassarre Peruzzi built this palazzo for the Massimo family, whose home had been destroyed in the 1527 Sack of Rome. Peruzzi displayed great ingenuity in dealing with an awkwardly shaped site. The previous building had stood on the ruined Theatre of Domitian, which created a curve in the great processional Via Papalis. Peruzzi's convex colonnaded façade follows the line of the street. His originality is also evident in the small square upper windows, the courtyard and the stuccoed vestibule. A single column from the theatre has been set up in the piazza.

The Massimo family traced its origins to Quintus Fabius Maximus, conqueror of Hannibal in the 3rd century BC, and their coat of arms is borne by an infant Hercules. Over the years this family dynasty produced many great Humanists, and in the 19th century, it was a Massimo who negotiated peace with Napoleon. On 16 March each year the family chapel opens to the public for a few hours (7am–1pm) to commemorate young

↑ The courtyard of the 16th-century Palazzo Massimo alle Colonne, designed by Baldassare Peruzzi

Paolo Massimo's resurrection from the dead by San Filippo Neri in 1538.

Pasquino

⚲ T3 ⌂ Piazza di Pasquino ▦ 40, 46, 62, 64, 70, 81, 87, 116, 492, 628

This rough chunk of marble is all that now remains of a Hellenistic group, probably representing the incident in Homer's *Iliad* in which Menelaus shields the body of the slain Patroclus. For years it lay as a stepping stone in a muddy medieval street until it was erected on this corner in 1501, near the shop of an outspoken cobbler named Pasquino. Freedom of speech was not encouraged in papal Rome, so the cobbler wrote out his satirical comments on current events and attached them to the statue.

Other Romans followed suit, hanging their maxims and verses on the statue by

night to escape punishment. Despite the wrath of the authorities, the sayings of the "talking statue" (renamed Pasquino) were part of popular culture up until the 19th century. Anonymous political maxims were hung on other statues, too. Sometimes satirical poems are still stuck onto the Pasquino statue.

Via del Governo Vecchio

⚲ S3 ▦ 40, 46, 62, 64

The street takes its name from Palazzo del Governo Vecchio, which was the seat of papal government in the 17th and 18th centuries. Once part of the Via Papalis, which led from the Lateran to St Peter's, the street is lined with 15th- and 16th-century houses and small workshops. Particularly interesting are those at No. 104 and No. 106. The small palazzo at No. 123 was once thought to have been the home of the architect Bramante. Opposite is Palazzo del Governo Vecchio. It is also known as Palazzo Nardini, from the name of its founder, which is inscribed, along with the date 1477, on the first-floor windows.

Sant'Andrea della Valle

📍 U4 🏛 Piazza Sant'Andrea della Valle
📞 06-6861339 🚌 H, 40, 46, 62, 64, 70, 81, 87, 116, 186, 492, 628 🚋 8
🕐 7:30am–12:30pm & 4:30–7:30pm daily

The church is the scene of the first act of Puccini's opera Tosca. Opera fans will not find the Attavanti Chapel a mere poetic invention. The real church still has much to recommend it – the impressive façade shows the flamboyant Baroque style at its best. Inside, a golden light filters through high windows, showing off the gilded interior. Here lie the two popes of the Sienese Piccolomini family: on the left of the central nave is the tomb of Pius II, the first Humanist pope (reigned 1458–64); Pope Pius III lies opposite – he reigned for less than a month in 1503.

The church is famous for its beautiful dome, which is the largest in Rome after St Peter's. It was built by Carlo Maderno in 1622–5 and was painted with splendid frescoes by Domenichino and Giovanni Lanfranco. The latter's extravagant style, to be seen in the dome fresco Glory of Paradise, won him most of the commission, and the jealous Domenichino is said to have tried to kill his colleague. He failed, but Domenichino's jealousy was unnecessary, as shown by his two beautiful paintings of scenes from the life of St Andrew around the apse and altar. In the Strozzi Chapel, built in the style of Michelangelo, the altar has copies of the Leah and Rachel by Michelangelo in San Pietro in Vincoli.

Palazzo Braschi

📍 T3 🏛 Piazza San Pantaleo 10 📞 06-6710 8303 🚌 40, 46, 62, 64, 70, 81, 87, 116, 186, 492, 628 🕐 10am–7pm Tue-Sun (ticket office closes at 6pm)

The last Roman palazzo to be built for the family of a pope, Palazzo Braschi was erected in the late 18th century for Pope Pius VI Braschi's nephews. Architect Cosimo Morelli gave the building its imposing façade overlooking the piazza.

The palazzo now houses the municipal Museo di Roma, with exhibits illustrating life in Rome from medieval times to the 19th century.

EAT

Lo Zozzone

A Roman institution, this cosy place serves delicious pizza bianca with an array of fillings from mozzarella to artichoke, plus tasty pasta dishes and crisp Roman-style pizza.

📍 T3 🏛 Via del Teatro Pace 32
📞 06-6880 8575

Osteria del Pegno

This romantic little restaurant with low lighting can be found on the ground floor of a 15th-century palazzo and offers a menu of perfectly executed Italian dishes. Complimentary limoncello and homemade biscuits round off a meal nicely.

📍 S2 🏛 Vicolo Montevecchio 8
📞 06-6880 7025

San Salvatore in Lauro

📍 S2 🏛 Piazza San Salvatore in Lauro 15 📞 06-687 5187 🚌 70, 81, 87, 116, 186, 280, 492 🕐 9am–noon & 3–7pm daily

Named "in Lauro" after the laurel grove that grew here in ancient times, this church was built at the end of the 1500s by Ottaviano Mascherino. The bell tower and sacristy were 18th-century additions by Nicola Salvi, famous for the Trevi Fountain.

The church contains the first great altarpiece by the 17th-century artist Pietro da Cortona, *The Birth of Jesus*, in the first chapel to the right.

The adjacent convent of San Giorgio includes a frescoed refectory and the monument to Pope Eugenius IV (reigned 1431–47), moved here when the old St Peter's was pulled down. An extravagant Venetian, Eugenius would willingly spend thousands of ducats on his gold tiara, but requested a "simple, lowly burial place" near his predecessor Pope Eugenius III.

In 1669 San Salvatore in Lauro became the seat of a pious association, the Confraternity of the Piceni, who were inhabitants of the Marche region. Fanatically loyal to the pope, the Piceni were employed as papal soldiers and tax collectors.

Palazzo Altemps

📍 T2 🏛 Via di Sant' Apollinare 46 📞 06-3996 7700 🚌 70, 81, 87, 116, 200, 492, 628 🕐 9am–7:45pm Tue–Sun (last adm: 1 hour before closing) 🔒 1 Jan, 25 Dec

An extraordinary collection of Classical sculpture is housed in this branch of the Museo Nazionale Romano. The palazzo was originally built for Girolamo Riario, nephew of Pope Sixtus IV, in 1480 and was restored as a museum in the 1990s. The Riario coat of arms can still be seen in the janitor's room. In the popular uprising that followed the pope's death in 1484, the building was sacked and Girolamo fled the city.

In 1568 the palazzo was bought by Cardinal Marco Sittico Altemps, and it was renovated by Martino Longhi the Elder in the 1570s. He added the great belvedere, crowned with obelisks and a marble unicorn.

The Altemps family were ostentatious collectors; the courtyard and its staircase are lined with ancient sculptures. These form part of the museum's collection, together with the Ludovisi collection of ancient sculptures, which was previously housed in the Museo Nazionale Romano in the Baths of Diocletian. On the first floor, at the far end of the courtyard, visitors can admire the Painted Loggia, dating from 1595. The Ludovisi throne, a Greek original carved in the 5th century BC, is on the same floor. In the Salone del Camino is the powerful statue *Galatian's Suicide*, a marble Roman replica of a group originally made in bronze in ancient Greece.

Nearby is the Ludovisi Sarcophagus, dating from the 3rd century AD.

SHOP

Delfina Delettrez

A scion of the Fendi dynasty, Delettrez is a jeweller whose bold and distinctive designs are beautifully arrayed in this sparkling little boutique, which is designed to resemble a jewellery box.

📍 T3 🏛 Via del Governo Vecchio 67 🌐 delfina delettrez.com

Museo Napoleonico

📍 T2 🏛 **Piazza di Ponte Umberto 1** 🚌 70, 81, 87, 116, 186, 280, 492 ⏰ 10am–6pm Tue–Sun 🚫 1 Jan, 1 May, 25 Dec 🌐 museonapoleonico.it

This free museum is dedicated to Napoleon Bonaparte and his family. Items that belonged to Napoleon himself include an Indian shawl he wore during his exile on St Helena.

After Napoleon's death in 1821 the pope allowed many of the Bonaparte family to settle in Rome, including his sister Pauline who married the Roman Prince Camillo Borghese. The museum has a cast of her right breast, made by Canova in 1805 as a study for his statue of her as a reclining Venus, now in the Galleria Borghese. Portraits and personal effects of other members of the family are on display, including uniforms, court dresses and a penny-farthing bicycle that belonged to Prince Eugène, the son of Emperor Napoleon III.

The collection was assembled in 1927 by the Counts Primoli, the sons of Napoleon Charles's sister, Carlotta.

The palace next door, in Via Zanardelli, houses the Racolta Praz (open Thu & Fri), a huge selection of *objets d'art*, paintings and furniture. Dating from the 17th and 18th centuries, they were collected by the art historian and literary critic Mario Praz.

Chiesa Nuova

📍 S3 🏛 **Piazza della Chiesa Nuova** 📞 06-687 5289 🚌 40, 46, 62, 64 ⏰ 7:30am–noon & 4:30–7pm daily

San Filippo Neri (St Philip Neri) is the most appealing of the Counter-Reformation saints. An unconventional reformer, he required his noble Roman followers to humble themselves in public – for example by setting noblemen to work as labourers on building his church. With the help of Pope Gregory XIII, his church was constructed in place of an old medieval church and it has been known ever since as the Chiesa Nuova (new church).

Begun in 1575 by Matteo da Città di Castello and continued by Martino Longhi the Elder, it was consecrated in 1599 (but the façade, by Fausto Rughesi, was only finished in 1606). Against San Filippo's wishes, the interior was decorated after his death; Pietro da Cortona frescoed the nave, dome and apse, taking nearly 20 years. There are also three paintings by Rubens: *Madonna and Angels; Saints Domitilla, Nereus and Achilleus;* and *Saints Gregory, Maurus and Papias.* San Filippo is buried in his own chapel, to the left of the altar.

The grand façades of the Oratorio dei Filippini (left) and Chiesa Nuova (right) ↓

PIAZZA DI SPAGNA
AND VILLA BORGHESE

The triangle of streets between Piazza del Popolo and Piazza di Spagna are studded with designer boutiques, bijou cosmetics shops, art galleries, antiques shops and upmarket delicatessens. It's an area in which to wander, window-shop and people-watch in between a little leisurely sightseeing. Via del Corso is full of chain shops, transforming into a human river at peak times. For respite, head to the Villa Borghese park, with its green lawns, shady pines, boating lake, museums and cafés.

The lush expanse of Villa Borghese, Rome's green lung ↓

The Spanish Steps with azaleas in full bloom and the church of Trinità dei Monti

PIAZZA DI SPAGNA

📍 H3 🚌 116, 117, 119 Ⓜ Spagna

Shaped like a crooked bow tie and surrounded by tall, shuttered houses painted in muted shades of ochre, pink and cream, Piazza di Spagna is the most famous square in Rome.

The square was long the haunt of expatriates and foreign visitors. In the 17th century the Spanish embassy was here, and the area around it was deemed to be Spanish territory – anyone who unwittingly trespassed was in danger of being dragooned into the Spanish army. In the 18th and 19th centuries the square stood at the heart of the main hotel district, attracting visitors from all over the world. Today the piazza is thronged with people all day and, in summer, most of the night. The church at the top of the steps, Trinità dei Monti, founded by the French in 1485, is famous for its breathtaking views.

Fontana della Barcaccia

Designed either by Gian Lorenzo Bernini or his father, Pietro, this fountain was an ingenious solution to the fact that the water pressure on the square was so low that spectacular cascades were not possible. Instead, the fountain represents a sinking boat, lying half submerged in a shallow pool. Pope Urban VIII Barberini commissioned the fountain in 1627.

EAT

Babington's Tea Rooms
These old-fashioned tea rooms were opened in 1896 by Englishwoman Anna Maria Babington to serve homesick British travellers with scones and tea. The menu today also includes burgers, salads, scrambled eggs, muffins and cakes. It is open for breakfast, lunch and dinner.

📍 H3 🏛 Piazza di Spagna 23
🌐 babingtons.com

€€€

↑ The dome of Raphael's Chigi Chapel, with mosaics showing God as creator of the seven heavenly bodies

SANTA MARIA DEL POPOLO

📍 G2 🏠 Piazza del Popolo 12 🚌 117, 119, 490, 495, 926 🚋 2 Ⓜ Flaminio 🕐 Check website for visiting times; no visits during Mass 🌐 santamariadelpopolo.it

Occupying the site where, according to legend, Nero was buried, this early Renaissance church was commissioned by Pope Sixtus IV della Rovere in 1472. It is one of Rome's greatest stores of artistic treasures.

Among the artists who worked on the building were Andrea Bregno and Pinturicchio. Later additions were made by Bramante and Bernini. Many illustrious families have chapels here, all decorated with appropriate splendour. The Della Rovere Chapel has delightful frescoes by Pinturicchio, the Cerasi Chapel has two Caravaggio master-pieces, but the finest of all is the Chigi Chapel designed by Raphael in 1513–16 for his patron, the banker Agostino Chigi. The most striking of the church's many Renaissance tombs are the two by Andrea Sansovino behind the main altar.

↑ Behind the altar, the stained-glass windows by the French artist Guillaume de Marcillat were the first in Rome.

VILLA BORGHESE

📍G2 🚪Entrances at Piazzale Flaminio, Porta Pinciana & Pincio Gardens 🚌52, 53, 88, 116, 490, 495 🚊3, 19

One of Rome's largest parks, Villa Borghese was laid out in the early 17th century by Cardinal Scipione Borghese, the pleasure-loving nephew of Pope Paul V.

A keen art collector, Scipione Borghese amassed one of Europe's finest collections of paintings, sculptures and antiquities. The young Bernini created many of his loveliest sculptures for Scipione, many of which are still displayed in the Galleria Borghese (formerly called Casino Borghese), created specifically to house the collection. Borghese was also a patron of Caravaggio. The park was redesigned in the 18th century by Scottish landscape artist Jacob More, with artificial lakes and Neo-Classical temples. In 1903 the park became the property of the Italian state and was opened to the general public. A replica of Shakespeare's Globe Theatre was added in 2003.

↓ Rowing on the lake in the Villa Borghese gardens

EAT

Casina del Lago
This charming little café next to the Museo Carlo Bilotti has great outdoor seating on a terrace (heated in winter), overlooking the lake. Open from 9am until sunset, it offers simple pizzas, pasta and rice dishes, salads and sandwiches, along with coffees, wine, cakes and pastries.

📍H2 🚪Viale dell'Aranciera 2
📞06-8535 2623
🚫Mon in winter

€€€

Did You Know?

Bikes, rollerskates, go-karts and boats are all for hire in the park.

VILLA GIULIA

📍 G1 🏠 Piazzale di Villa Giulia 9 🚌 52, 926 to Viale Bruno Buozzi; 88, 490, 495 to Viale Washington 🚋 3, 19 to Piazza Thorvaldsen 🕐 9am–8pm Tue–Sun (last adm: 6:30pm) 🌐 villagiulia.beniculturali.it

Since 1889 Villa Giulia has housed the Museo Nazionale Etrusco, with its outstanding collection of pre-Roman antiquities from central Italy. It holds the most important collection of Etruscan art in Italy.

Built as a country retreat for Pope Julius III in the 16th century, Villa Giulia was designed by exceptional architects: Vignola (designer of the Gesù), Vasari and the sculptor Ammannati. Michelangelo also contributed. The villa's main features are its façade, the courtyard and garden and the nymphaeum.

Etruscan Finds

Etruria was not a nation, but a federation of politically and economically independent cities in central Italy. The Etruscans were energetic traders – their wealth was based on prodigious natural resources of metals. If the finds from the tombs of the wealthy are any indication, they had a voracious appetite for the beautiful artifacts produced by their Greek and Phoenician trading partners. Tomb finds include the elaborately decorated chalices, wine jugs and kraters

↑ Sarcophagus of the Spouses (room 12), a 6th-century BC terracotta master-piece from Cerveteri, showing a dead couple at the eternal banquet

that may have graced Etruscan banqueting tables; mirrors and jewellery; and some extra-ordinary home accessories including a lion-foot candelabra. Artifacts on display come from most of the major excavations in Tuscany and Lazio. Rooms 1–13b and 30–40 are arranged by site and include Vulci, Todi, Veio and Cerveteri, while the remaining rooms are devoted to important objects that have been returned after being illegally excavated and sold, as well as private collections that have been donated to the museum.

←

The beautiful portico of Villa Giulia with frescoes by Pietro Venale, leading to the courtyard

EXPERIENCE MORE

Sant'Andrea delle Fratte

📍H4 🏛Via Sant'Andrea delle Fratte 1 📞06-679 3191 🚌116, 117 Ⓜ Spagna 🕐Summer: 6:30am-12:30pm & 4:30-8pm; winter: 6:15am-1pm & 4-7pm

When Sant'Andrea delle Fratte was built in the 1100s, this was the northernmost edge of Rome. Though the church is now firmly within the city, its name (*fratte* means "thickets") recalls its original setting.

The church was completely rebuilt in the 17th century, partly by Borromini. His bell tower and dome are notable for the complex concave and convex surfaces. The bell tower is particularly fanciful, with angel caryatids, flaming torches, and exaggerated scrolls like semi-folded hearts supporting a spiky crown.

In 1842, the Virgin Mary appeared in the church to a Jewish banker, who promptly converted to Christianity and became a missionary. Inside, the chapel of the Miraculous Madonna is the first thing you notice. The church is better known, however, for the angels that Borromini's rival, Bernini, carved for the Ponte

Sant'Angelo. Pope Clement IX declared they were too lovely to be exposed to the weather, so they remained with Bernini's family until 1729, when they were moved to the church.

Villa Medici

📍G3 🏛Accademia di Francia a Roma, Viale Trinità dei Monti 1 🚌117, 119 Ⓜ Spagna 🕐9:30am-6:30pm Tue-Sun for guided visits 🌐villamedici.it

Superbly positioned on the Pincio hill above Piazza di Spagna, this 16th-century villa has kept the name it assumed when Cardinal Ferdinando de' Medici bought it in 1576. From the terrace you can look across the city to Castel Sant'Angelo, from where Queen Christina of Sweden is said to have fired the large cannon ball which now sits in the basin of the fountain. The villa's most famous resident was Galileo, who was imprisoned here for falling foul of the Inquisition in 1630–33.

The villa is home to the French Academy, which was founded by Louis XIV in 1666 with the aim of giving a few select painters the chance to study in Rome. Nicolas Poussin was one of the first advisers to

the Academy, Ingres was a director, and former students include Jean-Honoré Fragonard and François Boucher.

It is now used for concerts and exhibitions. Guided tours take in the landscaped gardens and frescoed rooms. A highlight is the Stanza degli Uccelli.

Palazzo di Propaganda Fide

📍H4 🏛Via di Propaganda 1 📞06-6988 0266 🚌116, 117 Ⓜ Spagna

The Jesuit Congregation for the Propagation of the Faith was founded in 1622. Though Bernini had originally been commissioned to create their headquarters, Innocent X, who became pope in 1644, preferred the style of Borromini, who was asked to continue. His extraordinary west façade, completed in 1662, is striped with broad pilasters, between which the first-floor windows bend in and the central bay bulges. A rigid band divides its floors, and the cornice above the convex central bay swerves inwards. The more you look at it, the more restless it seems; a sign perhaps of the increasing unhappiness of the architect who committed suicide in 1667.

All Saints

📍 J2 🏛 Via del Babuino 153B 📞 06-3600 1881 🚌 117, 119 🕐 8:30am–7pm daily

In 1816 the pope gave English residents and visitors the right to hold Anglican services in Rome, but it was not until the early 1880s that they acquired a site to build their own church. The architect was G E Street, who is best known in Britain for his Neo-Gothic churches and the Royal Courts of Justice in London. The style of All Saints is also Victorian Neo-Gothic, and although the interior is splendidly decorated with different coloured Italian marbles, it has a very English air. Street also designed St-Paul's-within-the-Walls in Via Nazionale, whose interior is a jewel of British Pre-Raphaelite art.

The street on which All Saints stands got its name from the Fontana del Sileno, notorious for its ugliness, and nicknamed "baboon".

Ara Pacis

📍 G3 🏛 Lungotevere in Augusta 🚌 70, 81, 117, 119, 186, 628 🕐 9:30am–7:30pm daily (last adm: 6:30pm) 📅 1 Jan, 1 May, 25 Dec 🌐 arapacis.it

Reconstructed at considerable expense over the course of many years, the Ara Pacis (Altar of Peace) is one of the most significant monuments of ancient Rome. It celebrates the peace created throughout the Mediterranean area by Emperor Augustus following his victorious campaigns in Gaul and Spain. The monument was commissioned by the Senate in 13 BC and completed four years later. It was positioned in such a way that the shadow of the huge obelisk sundial on Campus Martius would fall upon it on Augustus's birthday.

Forming a square enclosure on a low platform with the altar in the centre, the Ara Pacis is decorated with magnificent friezes and reliefs carved in Carrara marble. The reliefs on the north and south walls depict a procession that took place on 4 July 13 BC, in which the members of the emperor's family can be identified, ranked by their position in the succession. At the time, the heir apparent was Marcus Agrippa, husband of Augustus's daughter Julia. All the portraits in the relief are carved with extraordinary realism, even the innocent toddler clinging to his mother's skirts.

The history of the rediscovery of the Ara Pacis dates back to the 16th century, when the first panels were unearthed at nearby Via in Lucina. One of the sections ended up in Paris, while another found its way to Florence. Further discoveries were made in the late 19th century, when archaeologists finally realized just what they had found. The monument as it appears today has all been pieced together since 1938, with some parts original and other parts reproductions. The American architect Richard Meier designed a dedicated glass building to house the entire structure, which opened in 2006.

The large Piazza del Popolo at sunset

Piazza del Popolo

📍 G2 🚌 117, 119, 490, 495, 926 🚋 2
Ⓜ Flaminio

A vast cobbled oval standing at the apex of the triangle of roads known as the Trident, Piazza del Popolo forms a grand symmetrical ante-chamber to the heart of Rome. Twin Neo-Classical façades stand on either side of the Porta del Popolo; an Egyptian obelisk rises in the centre; and the matching domes and porticoes of Santa Maria dei Miracoli and Santa Maria in Montesanto flank the beginning of Via del Corso.

Although it is now one of the most unified squares in Rome, Piazza del Popolo evolved gradually over the centuries. In 1589 the great town-planning pope, Sixtus V, had the obelisk erected in the centre by Domenico Fontana. Over 3,000 years old, the obelisk in Piazza del Popolo was originally brought to Rome by Augustus to adorn the Circus Maximus after the conquest of Egypt. Almost a century later Pope Alexander VII commissioned Carlo Rainaldi to build the twin Santa Marias. In the 19th century the piazza was turned into a grandiose oval by Giuseppe Valadier, the designer of the Pincio Gardens.

In contrast to the piazza's air of ordered rationalism, many of the events staged here were barbaric. In the 18th and 19th cen-turies, public executions were held. Condemned men were sometimes hammered to death by repeated blows to the temples. The last time a criminal was executed in this way was in 1826, even though the guillotine had by then been adopted as a more scientific means of execution.

The riderless horse races from the piazza down Via del Corso were scarcely more humane: the perfor-mance of the runners was enhanced by feeding the horses stimulants, wrap-ping them in nail-studded ropes and letting off fireworks at their heels.

To the north of the piazza, Via Flaminia, built in 220 BC to connect Rome with Italy's Adriatic coast, enters the city at Porta del Popolo, a grand 16th-century gate built on the orders of Pope Pius IV de' Medici. The architect, Nanni di Baccio Bigio, modelled it on a Roman triumphal arch. The outer face has statues of St Peter and St Paul on either side and a Medici coat of arms. A century later, Pope Alexander VII commission-ed Bernini to decorate the inner face to celebrate the arrival in Rome in 1655 of Queen Christina of Sweden after abdi-cating her throne and converting to Roman Catholicism the previous year. Lesser visitors were often delayed while customs officers rifled their luggage. The only way to speed things up was with a bribe.

Via Condotti

🅖 G3 & 4 🚌 81, 116, 117, 119, 492 and many routes along via del Corso or stopping at Piazza San Silvestro Ⓜ Spagna

Named after the conduits that carried water to the Baths of Agrippa near the Pantheon, Via Condotti is now home to the most traditional of Rome's designer clothes shops. Stores selling shoes and other leather goods are also well represented. The street is popular for early evening strolls, when elegant Italians mingle with casually dressed tourists. The street is home to Gucci, Louis Vuitton, Dolce e Gabbana, Bulgari, Salvatore Ferragamo, Prada, Burberry and Trussardi, among other designer boutiques.

Pincio Gardens

🅖 G2 🅐 Il Pincio 🚌 117, 119, 490, 495, 628, 926 🚋 2 Ⓜ Flaminio

The Pincio Gardens lie above Piazza del Popolo on a hillside that has been so skilfully terraced and richly planted with trees that, from below, the zig-zagging road climbing to the gardens is virtually invisible. In ancient Roman times, there were magnificent gardens on the Pincio Hill. The present gardens were designed in the early 19th century by Giuseppe Valadier (who

GREAT VIEW
Pincio Gardens

Approach the Pincio Gardens from the grounds of Villa Borghese above the Pincio, or along Viale della Trinità dei Monti. The panoramic views of Rome are particularly beautiful at sunset.

also redesigned the Piazza del Popolo). The broad avenues, lined with umbrella pines, palm trees and evergreen oaks soon became a fashionable place to stroll, and even in the 20th century such diverse characters as Gandhi and Mussolini,

Richard Strauss and King Farouk of Egypt patronized the Casina Valadier, an exclusive café and restaurant in the grounds. From the Pincio's main square, Piazzale Napoleone I, the panoramic views of Rome stretch from the Monte Mario to the Janiculum.

One of the most striking features of the park itself is an Egyptian-style obelisk which Emperor Hadrian erected on the tomb of his favourite, the male slave Antinous. After the slave's premature death (according to some accounts he died saving the emperor's life), Hadrian deified him.

Marble busts of many historical Italian and other European figures line the paths of the gardens. The 19th-century water clock on Via dell'Orologio was designed by a Dominican monk. It was displayed at the Paris Exhibition of 1889.

Casa di Goethe

📍 G3 🏠 Via del Corso 18 🚌 117, 119, 490, 495, 628, 926 🚊 2 Ⓜ Flaminio ⏰ 10am-6pm daily 🌐 casadigoethe.it

The German poet, dramatist and novelist Johann

Via Condotti, the famous shopping street leading to the Spanish Steps

Wolfgang von Goethe (1749–1832) lived in this house from 1786 until 1788 and worked on a journal that eventually formed part of his travel book *The Italian Journey*. Rome's noisy street life irritated him, especially during Carnival time. He was a little perturbed by the number of murders in his neighbourhood, but Rome energized him and his book became one of the most influential ever written about Italy

---

Santi Ambrogio e Carlo al Corso

📍 G3 🏠 Via del Corso 437 📞 06-682 8101 🚌 81, 117, 492, 628, 926 ⏰ 7am-7pm daily

This church belonged to the Lombard community in Rome, and is dedicated to two canonized bishops of Milan, Lombardy's capital. In 1471 Pope Sixtus IV gave the Lombards a church, and they dedicated it to Sant'Ambrogio, who died in 397. Then in 1610, when Carlo Borromeo was canonized, the church was rebuilt in his honour. Most of the work on the new church was carried out by father and son Onorio and Martino Longhi, but the fine dome is by Pietro da Cortona. The altarpiece by Carlo Maratta (1625–1713) is the *Gloria dei Santi Ambrogio e Carlo.*

An ambulatory leads behind the altar to a chapel housing the heart of San Carlo, which is held in a richly decorated reliquary.

Santa Maria dei Miracoli and Santa Maria in Montesanto

📍 G2 🏠 Piazza del Popolo 🚌 117, 119, 490, 495, 628, 926 🚊 2 Ⓜ Flaminio
Santa Maria dei Miracoli: 📞 06-361 0250 ⏰ 7am-12:30pm & 4-7:30pm daily
Santa Maria in Montesanto: 📞 06-361 0594 ⏰ 5:30-8pm Mon-Fri, 11am-1:30pm Sun

The two churches at the south end of Piazza del Popolo were designed by the architect Carlo Rainaldi (1611–91), the plans were revised by Bernini and it was Carlo Fontana who eventually completed the project. To provide a focal point for the piazza, the churches had to appear symmetrical. Although the two churches appear identical at first glance, there are differences if you look carefully. The site on the left was narrower. Hence, Rainaldi gave Santa Maria dei Miracoli (on the right) a circular dome and Santa Maria in Montesanto an oval one to squeeze it into the narrower site, while keeping the sides of the supporting drums that face the piazza identical.

CAMPO DE' FIORI

The area between Corso Vittorio Emanuele and the Tiber River, Campo de' Fiori is dominated by the morning food market in Campo de' Fiori itself. In and around the square the neighbourhood's culinary traditions have spawned some of the city's most authentic places to eat Roman food – some long-established and some contemporary. The area gets very lively at sundown, with students, locals and tourists flooding its eateries and bars.

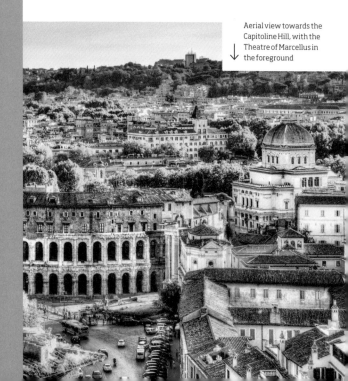

Aerial view towards the Capitoline Hill, with the Theatre of Marcellus in the foreground

↑ Statue of Giordano Bruno in Campo de' Fiori

↑ The busy open-air market in Campo de' Fiori

CAMPO DE' FIORI

📍 T4 🚌 116 and routes to Largo di Torre Argentina or Corso Vittorio Emanuele II

A lively square since medieval times, Campo de' Fiori bursts with colour during the morning market, and again after dark when its restaurants and bars make it a centre of Roman nightlife.

💬 INSIDER TIP
Shopping

The streets around the piazza, named for the medieval artisans who traded there, are lined with boutiques. One of the best is Via de' Giubbonari ("jerkin-makers"), which has many chic clothes shops.

Occupying the site of a meadow in ancient times behind the vast structure of the Teatro di Pompeo, Campo de' Fiori became the bustling, raffish – and at times rough – heart of Renaissance Rome, populated by artists, craftsmen and courtesans, and packed with cheap inns. Murders were not uncommon – Caravaggio killed his opponent on the piazza after losing a game of tennis, and the goldsmith Benvenuto Cellini murdered a business rival on nearby Via della Moretta. Today the square is home to Rome's most central fresh produce market between 7am and 1:30pm Monday to Saturday.

Giordano Bruno Monument

In the centre of Campo de' Fiori is a statue of the philosopher Giordano Bruno. A former Catholic priest who dabbled in Calvinism and Lutheranism before being excommunicated by both, Bruno eventually concluded that philosophy and magic were superior to religion. He was tried for heresy and burned at the stake in 1600. His hooded statue is a grim reminder of the executions by the Inquisition that took place in the piazza.

EXPERIENCE MORE

Teatro di Pompeo

📍 T4 🏛 Da Pancrazio, Piazza del Biscione 92 🚌 116 and routes to Largo Torre Argentina or Corso Vittorio Emanuele II

A hint of Pompey's 55 BC theatre is evident in the curve of medieval Largo del Pollaro. The theatre could seat 17,000 people. Traces of it are visible in the ancient travertine corridors of the Pancrazio restaurant where you can see early examples of *opus reticulatum* – small square blocks of tufa (porous rock) set diagonally as a facing for a concrete wall.

Palazzo Spada

📍 T5 🏛 Piazza Capo di Ferro 13 📞 06-683 2409 🚌 23, 116, 280 and routes to Largo di Torre Argentina 🚋 8 🕐 8:30am–7:30pm Wed-Mon (last adm: 7pm)

This majestic palazzo, built around 1550 for Cardinal Capo di Ferro, has an elegant stuccoed courtyard and façade decorated with reliefs evoking Rome's glorious past. Cardinal Bernardino Spada, who lived here in the 17th century with his brother Virginio (also a cardinal), hired architects Bernini and Borromini to work on the building. The brothers' whimsical delight in false perspectives resulted in a colonnaded gallery by Borromini that appears four times longer than it really is.

The cardinals also amassed a superb private collection of paintings, which is now on display in the Galleria Spada. The collection, housed in four rooms, features 16th- and 17th-century pieces by a wide range of artists, including Rubens, Dürer, Guercino, Guido Reni and Artemesia Gentileschi. The most significant of the artworks on display include *The Visitation* by Andrea del Sarto (1486–1530), *Cain and Abel* by Giovanni Lanfranco (1582–1647) and *The Death of Dido* by Guercino (1591–1666). The palace is also the seat of government offices.

Palazzo del Monte di Pietà

📍 T5 🏛 Piazza del Monte di Pietà 33 📞 06-684 42001 🚌 116 and routes to Largo di Torre Argentina or Corso Vittorio Emanuele II 🚋 8

The Monte, as it is known, is a public institution, founded in 1539 by Pope Paul III Farnese as a pawnshop to staunch the usury then rampant in the city. The building still has offices and auction rooms for the sale of unredeemed goods.

The stars with diagonal bands on the huge central plaque decorating the façade are the coat of arms of Pope Clement VIII Aldobrandini, added when Carlo Maderno enlarged the palace in the 17th century. The clock under the bell tower on the left was added towards the end of the 18th century.

→ Borromini's forced-perspective colonnaded gallery at Palazzo Spada

The 17th-century altarpiece depicting the *Holy Trinity* by Guido Reni in Santissima Trinità dei Pellegrini

Within, the chapel (which is open only for accredited groups; phone ahead) is a jewel of Baroque architecture, adorned with gilded stucco, marble panelling and reliefs. It is a perfect setting for the sculptures by Domenico Guidi – a bust of San Carlo Borromeo and a relief of the *Pietà*. There are also splendid reliefs by Giovanni Battista Théudon and Pierre Legros of biblical scenes illustrating the charitable nature of the institution.

Sant'Eligio degli Orefici

📍 S4 🏛 Via di Sant'Eligio 8A ☎ 06-686 8260 🚌 23, 40, 46, 62, 64, 116, 280 🕐 9:30am-1pm Mon-Fri (ring bell first at Via di Sant'Eligio 7) 🚫 Aug

The name of the church marks the fact that it was commissioned by a rich corporation of goldsmiths (*orefici*) in the early 16th century. The original design was by Raphael, who, like his master Bramante, had acquired a sense of the grandiose from the remains of Roman antiquity. The influence of some of Bramante's works, such as the choir of Santa Maria del Popolo, is evident in the simple way the arches and pilasters define the structure of the walls. The cupola of Sant' Eligio is attributed to Baldassarre Peruzzi, while the façade was added in the early 17th century by Flaminio Ponzio.

Santissima Trinità dei Pellegrini

📍 T5 🏛 Via dei Pettinari 36A ☎ 06-686 8451 🚌 23, 116, 280 and routes to Largo di Torre Argentina 🚋 8 🕐 4-8pm Mon-Sat, 8am-1pm & 4-8pm Sun

The church was donated in the 16th century to a charitable organization founded by San Filippo Neri to care for the poor and sick. The 18th-century façade has niches with statues of the Evangelists by Bernardino Ludovisi. The interior, with Corinthian columns, ends in a horse-shoe vault and apse, dominated by Guido Reni's striking altarpiece of the Holy Trinity (1625). The frescoes in the lantern are also by Reni.

Other interesting paintings include *St Gregory the Great Freeing Souls from Purgatory* by Baldassarre Croce (third chapel to the left); Cavalier d'Arpino's *Virgin and Saints* (second chapel to the left); and a painting by Borgognone (1677) of the Virgin and recently canonized saints. In the sacristy are depictions of the nobility washing the feet of pilgrims, a custom started by San Filippo.

San Girolamo della Carità

📍S4 🏠Via di Monserrato 62A 📞06-687 9786 🚌23, 40, 46, 62, 64, 116, 280 🕐5-7pm Tue-Fri, 10am-1pm Sun

The church was built on a site incorporating the home of San Filippo Neri, the 16th-century saint from Tuscany who renewed Rome's spiritual and cultural life by his friendly, open approach to religion. He would have loved the frolicking putti shown around his statue in the Antamoro chapel dedicated to him – they would have reminded him of the Roman urchins he had cared for during his lifetime. The breathtaking Spada Chapel, designed by Borromini, is unique both as a work of art and as an illustration of the spirit of the Baroque age. All architectural elements are concealed so that the space of the chapel's interior is defined solely by decorative marble-work and statues. Veined jasper and precious multi-coloured marbles are sculpted to imitate flowery damask and velvet hangings. Even the altar rail is a long swag of jasper drapery held up by a pair of kneeling angels with wooden wings.

Although there are memorials to former members of the Spada family, oddly there is no indication as to which of the Spadas was responsible for endowing the chapel. It was probably art-lover Virgilio Spada, a follower of San Filippo Neri.

Palazzo Ricci

📍S4 🏠Piazza de' Ricci 🚌23, 40, 46, 62, 64, 116, 280, 870 🚫To the public

Palazzo Ricci was famous for its frescoed façade – now rather faded – originally painted in the 16th century by Polidoro da Caravaggio, a follower of Raphael.

In Renaissance Rome it was common to commission artists to decorate the outsides of houses with heroes of Classical antiquity. A fresco by a leading artist such as Polidoro, the inventor of this style of painting, was a conspicuous status symbol,

←

Via del Pellegrino and Via di Monserrato, as seen from Via dei Banchi Vecchi

in the nobility's attempts to outshine each other with their palazzi.

Palazzo Farnese

T4 **Piazza Farnese**
23, 116, 280 and routes to Corso Vittorio Emanuele II **For guided tours only (Mon, Wed & Fri in English, times vary); book online at least one week ahead** **inventerrome.com**

The prototype for numerous princely palaces, Palazzo Farnese was originally built for Cardinal Alessandro Farnese (who became Pope Paul III in 1534). He commissioned the greatest artists to work on it, starting with Antonio da Sangallo the Younger as architect in 1517. Michelangelo, who took over after him, contributed the great cornice and central window of the main façade, and the third level of the courtyard. The interior is decorated with frescoes by leading artists including Annibale Carracci and Daniele da Volterra.

Michelangelo had a plan for the Farnese gardens to be connected by a bridge to the Farnese home in Trastevere, Villa

Farnesina, but the scheme was unrealized. The palazzo was completed in 1589, on a less ambitious scale, by Giacomo della Porta. It is has been the home of the French Embassy since 1635.

Santa Maria in Monserrato

S4 **Via di Monserrato 115** **06-686 5865**
23, 40, 46, 62, 64, 116, 280 **5-7pm Sat, 8:30am-1pm & 3-7pm Sun. To arrange a visit Mon-Fri, call 06-688 9651**

The origins of the Spanish national church in Rome go back to 1506, when a hospice for Spanish pilgrims was begun by a brotherhood of the Virgin of Montserrat in Catalonia. Inside is Annibale Carracci's painting *San Diego de Alcalá* and a copy of a Sansovino statue of St James. Beautiful 15th-century tombs by Andrea Bregno and Luigi Capponi are in the courtyard and side chapels. Do not miss Bernini's bust of church benefactor Pedro Foix de Montoya in the annexe.

Did You Know?

Charles Barry used Palazzo Farnese as the model for London's Reform Club in 1841.

Piccola Farnesina

T4 **Corso Vittorio Emanuele II 168** **40, 46, 62, 64, 70, 81, 87, 116, 492** **Oct-May: 10am-4pm Tue-Sun; Jun-Sep: 1-7pm Tue-Sun** **museo barracco.it**

This miniature palazzo acquired its name from the lilies decorating its cornices that were mistakenly identified as part of the Farnese family crest. In fact they were part of the coat of arms of a French clergyman, Thomas Le Roy, for whom the palazzo was built in 1523.

The entrance is in a façade built to overlook Corso Vittorio Emanuele II when the road was built at the start of the 1900s. The original façade on the left of today's entrance is attributed to Antonio da Sangallo the Younger.

The Piccola Farnesina now houses the Museo Barracco, a sculpture collection assembled during the 19th century by the politician Baron Giovanni Barracco. A bust of the baron is in the courtyard. The collection includes an ancient Egyptian relief of the scribe Nofer, some Assyrian artifacts and, among the Etruscan exhibits, a delicate ceramic female head. On the first floor is the Greek collection with a head of Apollo.

Palazzo della Cancelleria

📍 T4 🏛 Piazza della Cancelleria 📞 06-6988 7566 🚌 40, 46, 62, 64, 70, 81, 87, 116, 492 Courtyard: 🕐 7:30am-8pm Mon-Sat, 9:30am-7pm Sun Sala Riaria and Salone dei Cento Giorni: 🕐 Tue pm & Sat am (call 06-6989 3405 at least a month in advance)

The palazzo, a prime example of Early Renaissance architecture, was begun in 1485. It was financed partly with the gambling winnings of Cardinal Raffaele Riario, who was in charge of the Papal Chancellery. Roses, the emblem of the Riario family, adorn the vaults and capitals of the beautiful Doric courtyard. The palazzo's interior was decorated after the Sack of Rome in 1527. Giorgio Vasari boasted that he had completed work on one enormous room in just 100 days (thus it was named Salone dei Cento Giorni); Michelangelo allegedly retorted: "It looks like it." Mannerist artists Perin del Vaga and Francesco Salviati frescoed the cardinal's rooms. The splendid Sala Riaria has a clock face painted by Baciccia. On the right of the palazzo's main entrance is the church of San Lorenzo in Damaso, founded by Pope Damasus (reigned 366–84). It was reconstructed in 1495.

Teatro Argentina

📍 U4 🏛 Largo di Torre Argentina 52 🚌 40, 46, 62, 64, 70, 81, 87, 186, 492, 810 🚋 8 🕐 Museum by appt only (call 06-0608) 🌐 teatrodiroma.net

One of Rome's most influential theatres was founded by the Sforza Cesarini family in 1732, though the façade dates from a century later. Many famous operas, including those of Verdi, were first performed here. In 1816 the theatre saw the ill-fated debut of Rossini's *Barber of Seville*, during which the composer insulted the unappreciative audience, who then pursued him hissing and jeering through the streets.

Santa Maria in Campitelli

📍 V5 🏛 Piazza di Campitelli 9 📞 06-6880 3978 🚌 40, 46, 62, 63, 64, 70, 87, 186, 780, 810 🕐 7am-7pm daily

In 17th-century Rome the plague could still strike fiercely and there were no reliable, effective remedies. Many Romans simply prayed for a cure to a sacred medieval icon of the Virgin, the Madonna del Portico. When a particularly lethal outbreak of plague abated in 1656, popular gratitude was so strong that a new church was built to house the icon.

The church, designed by Bernini's pupil Carlo Rainaldi, was completed in 1667. The main elements of the lively Baroque façade are the graceful columns, symbolizing the supporters of the true faith. Inside the church stands a fabulously ornate, gilded altar tabernacle with spiral columns, designed by Giovanni Antonio de Rossi to contain the image of the Virgin. The side chapels are decorated by some of Rome's finest

← The courtyard of the Renaissance Palazzo della Cancelleria

Baroque artists: Sebastiano Conca, Giovanni Battista Gaulli (known as Il Baciccia) and Luca Giordano.

Fontana delle Tartarughe

⚑ V5 ⌂ Piazza Mattei
🚌 46, 62, 63, 64, 70, 87, 186, 492, 810 🚋 8

The delightful Fontana delle Tartarughe (*tartarughe* means "tortoises") was commissioned by the Mattei family between 1581 and 1588 to decorate "their" piazza. The design was by Giacomo della Porta, but the fountain owes much of its charm to the four bronze youths each resting one foot on the head of a dolphin, sculpted by Taddeo Landini. Nearly a century after the fountain was built an unknown sculptor, possibly Bernini, added the tortoises to complete the composition.

San Carlo ai Catinari

⚑ U4 ⌂ Piazza B. Cairoli
📞 06-6830 7070 🚌 40, 46, 62, 64, 70, 81, 87, 186, 492, 810 🚋 8 🕐 7:30am–noon & 4-7pm daily

In 1620 Rome's Milanese congregation decided to honour Cardinal Carlo Borromeo, who was made a saint, with this great church. It was called "ai Catinari" on account of the many bowl-makers' (*catinari*) shops in the area surrounding the church. The solemn travertine façade was completed in 1638 by the Roman architect Soria. The 16th-century basilican plan is flanked by chapels. The St Cecilia Chapel was designed and decorated by Antonio Gherardi. The church's paintings and frescoes by Pietro da Cortona and Guido Reni depict the life and acts of San Carlo. The ornate crucifix on the sacristy altar is inlaid with marble and mother-of-pearl and is by the 16th-century sculptor Algardi.

Crypta Balbi

⚑ V4 ⌂ Via delle Botteghe Oscure
🕐 9am-7:45pm Tue-Sun 🌐 museo nazionale romano.beni culturali.it

Part of the Museo Nazionale Romano, Crypta Balbi is an inventive museum devoted to urban archaeology, and illustrates how a piece of land in central Rome has been used over the centuries. It stands on the remains of a theatre built in 13 BC, the ruins of which can still be seen. Further excavations revealed that in the 1st century AD the esedra (the curved auditorium) had been converted into what appears to have been a smart public lavatory, with marble seats. Then, it seems, the area went downhill, as in the 3rd century blocks of flats

(*insulae*) for the poor were constructed, one of them with a Mithraeum in the basement. By the 7th century the area had become a glassworks, evidenced by a huge dump of discarded glass.

←

The Ponte Fabricio footbridge that links the Ghetto to Tiber Island

San Nicola in Carcere

V5 **Via del Teatro di Marcello 46** **06-6830 7198** **44, 63, 81, 160, 170, 628, 780, 781** **10am-5pm daily Excavations: call 347-3811874 to book**

The medieval church of San Nicola in Carcere stands on the site of three Roman temples of the Republican era which were converted into a prison *(carcere)* in the Middle Ages. The temples of Juno, Spes and Janus faced a city gate leading from the Forum Holitorium, the city's vegetable and oil market, to the road down to the port on the Tiber. The underground excavations are well worth a visit. The columns embedded in the walls of the church belonged to two flanking temples whose platforms are now marked by lawns. The church was rebuilt in 1599, with a new façade by

Giacomo della Porta, and restored during the 19th century, but the bell tower and Roman columns, incorporated into the church's façade, are part of the original design.

Tiber Island

U5 **Isola Tiberina** **23, 63, 280, 780** **8**

In ancient times the island, which lay opposite the city's port, had large structures of white travertine at either end, built to resemble the stern and prow of a ship. Since 293 BC, when a temple was dedicated to Aesculapius, the god of healing and protector against the plague, the island has been associated with the sick. San Bartolomeo all'Isola, the church in the island's central piazza, was built on the ruins of the Temple of Aesculapius in the

10th century. Its bell tower is visible from across the river. From the Ghetto area you can reach the island by a footbridge, the Ponte Fabricio. The oldest original bridge over the Tiber still in use, it was built in 62 BC. In medieval times the Pierleoni and then the Caetani, two powerful families, controlled this strategic point by use of a tower, still *in situ*. The other bridge to the island, the Ponte Cestio, is inscribed with the names of the Byzantine emperors associated with its restoration in AD 370.

Theatre of Marcellus

V5 **Via del Teatro di Marcello** **06-0608** **44, 63, 81, 160, 170, 628, 780, 781** **9am-6pm daily (summer: to 7pm)**

The curved outer wall of this vast amphitheatre has supported generations of Roman buildings. It was built by Emperor Augustus (27 BC–AD 14), who dedicated it to Marcellus, his nephew and son-in-law, who had died aged 19 in 23 BC. The Middle Ages were a turbulent time of invasions and local conflicts and by the 13th century the theatre had been converted into the fortress of the Savelli family. In the 16th century Baldassarre Peruzzi built a great palace on the theatre ruins for the Orsini family. This included a garden that faced the Tiber.

Close to the theatre stand three Corinthian columns and a section of frieze. These are from the Temple of Apollo, which once housed many great works of art that the Romans had plundered from Greece in the 2nd century BC.

Portico of Octavia

Q V5 **A** Via del Portico d'Ottavia **🚌** 46, 62, 63, 64, 70, 87, 186, 780, 810

Built in honour of Octavia (the sister of Augustus and the abandoned wife of Mark Antony), this is the only surviving portico of what used to be the monumental piazza of Circus Flaminius. The rectangular portico enclosed temples dedicated to Jupiter and Juno, decorated with bronze statues. The part you see today is the great central atrium originally covered by marble facings. In the Middle Ages a great fish market and a church, Sant'Angelo in Pescheria, were built in the ruins of the portico. As the church was associated with the fishing activities of the nearby river port, aquatic flora and fauna feature in

many of its inlays. Links with the Tiber are also apparent in the stucco façade on the adjacent Fishmonger's Oratory, built in 1689. The church has a fresco of the Madonna and angels by the school of Benozzo Gozzoli.

San Giovanni dei Fiorentini

Q R2 **A** Via Acciaioli 2 **📞** 06-6889 2059 **🚌** 23, 40, 46, 62, 64, 116, 280, 870 **🕐** 7:25am–noon & 5-7pm daily

The church of St John of the Florentines was built for the large Florentine community in this area. Pope Leo X wanted it to be an expression of the cultural superiority of Florence over Rome. Started in the early 16th century, the church took over a century to build. The principal architect was Antonio da Sangallo the Younger, but many others contributed before Carlo Maderno's elongated cupola was finally completed in 1620. The present façade was added in the 18th century. The church was decorated mainly by Tuscan artists. One interesting exception is the 15th-century statue of San Giovannino by the Sicilian Mino del Reame in a niche above the sacristy. The spectacular high altar houses a marble group by Antonio Raggi, *The Baptism*

of Christ. The altar itself is by Borromini, who is buried in the church. The church also has a small museum of sacred art (open 9:30am–noon Mon–Sat).

EAT

Il Forno di Campo de' Fiori

This is the best place locally for a takeaway lunch: delicious *pizza bianca* stuffed with anything from mortadella to Nutella. Also try the delicious biscuits and pastries.

Q T4 **A** Vicolo del Gallo 14 **🌐** fornocampode fiori.com

Roscioli

This family-owned restaurant/deli is renowned for its wines, meats and cheeses. The antipasti and pasta dishes are particularly delicious.

Q T4 **A** Via dei Giubbonari 21 **🌐** salumeriaroscioli. com

QUIRINAL AND MONTI

A sprawling zone cut through by traffic-clogged Via Nazionale, Quirinal stretches downhill, encompassing the slopes of the Viminal – dominated by the august façade and sombre denizens of the Ministry of the Interior – and across to the Quirinal Hill. Here the Palazzo del Quirinale, residence of the Italian president, dominates a rather desolate piazza. Rome's most famous fountain, the Trevi, is nearby. For coffee, lunch, shopping or an *aperitivo*, head to the livelier, fashionable Monti district.

The splendid Galleria Colonna inside
↓ Palazzo Colonna

TREVI FOUNTAIN

◉H4 🚌52, 53, 61, 62, 63, 71, 80, 116, 119 and other routes along Via del Corso and Via del Tritone

Tucked away on a tiny piazza, this is the most famous – and the largest – fountain in Rome. Built in 1762 by Italian architect Nicola Salvi, in the flamboyant Rococo style, the Trevi Fountain is a travertine extravaganza of rearing seahorses, conch-blowing Tritons, craggy rocks and palm trees built into the side of the Palazzo Poli.

The fountain's waters come from the Acqua Vergine, a Roman aqueduct built in 19 BC and fed by springs 22 km (14 miles) from the city. Legend has it that the Acqua Vergine is named after a young virgin called Trivia who showed Roman engineers the location of a freshwater spring. The word Trevi is a corruption of her name. The fountain contains about 3 million litres (666,000 gallons) of water. Once reputed to be the sweetest water in Rome, it is now treated with chemicals. Legend has it that throwing a coin into the fountain guarantees a return to Rome.

Oceanus and Chariot pulled by Tritons and Horses

The central statue standing in a triumphal arch is of Oceanus, the personification of an enormous river encircling the world from which all streams of water are derived in ancient mythology. The statue was carved by Pietro Bracci, who took over work on the fountain after the death of Nicola Salvi, his long-time friend, in 1751. Oceanus's conch-shell chariot is powered by two horses steered by Tritons. One Triton struggles to master an unruly beast, while the other leads a far more docile animal. The horses were intended to symbolize the different moods of the sea.

LA CITTÀ DELL'ACQUA

In 2001 a stretch of the Acqua Vergine aqueduct (built in Augustan times and still feeding the Trevi Fountain) was revealed during restoration of an old cinema. Part of the underground archaeological area of "The City of Water" can now be visited, including the aqueduct and the ruins of an ancient Roman apartment block *(insula)* that was later converted into a single family home. Artifacts uncovered in the area are also on display.

↑ The Trevi Fountain illuminated at night

↑ Courtyard of the 19th-century Palazzo Massimo alle Terme, lined with statues

BATHS OF DIOCLETIAN

◉ L4 **☗** Terme di Diocleziano, Viale E de Nicola 79 **☎** 06-3996 7700 **☉** 9am-7:30pm Tue-Sun

Built under Emperor Diocletian between AD 298 and 306, this bath complex was the largest in ancient Rome. Parts were later converted into the church of Santa Maria degli Angeli e dei Martiri. The Baths now house the Museo Nazionale Romano's collection of funerary monuments and inscriptions. Highlights include a display about the history of writing and a section on amulets and magic.

PALAZZO MASSIMO ALLE TERME

◉ L4 **☗** Largo di Villa Peretti 1 **☎** 06-3996 7700 **🚌** H, 36, 38, 40, 64, 170 and other routes to Piazza del Cinquecento **q** Repubblica, Termini **☉** 9am-7:45pm Tue-Sun

The main site of the Museo Nazionale Romano, the airy 19th-century Palazzo Massimo alle Terme holds an exceptional collection of antiquities dating from the 2nd century BC to the end of the 4th century AD.

Founded in 1889, the museum contains one of the world's leading collections of Classical art, comprising frescoes, mosaics, statues and other artifacts found in Rome since 1870. The exhibits are beautifully displayed on several floors. The courtyard, with its portico of statues dappled with light and shade, is a wonderful introduction to this spectacular collection. The museum

has many highlights, but the exquisite frescoes from Livia's Villa are a particular must see.

The Museo Nazionale Romano has four sites. The other branches are in the Baths of Diocletian, just around the corner from Palazzo Massimo alle Terme *(see box)*, the Crypta Balbi and Palazzo Altemps. The same entry ticket is valid for all four sites for three consecutive days.

EXPERIENCE MORE

Castor and Pollux

📍J5 🏛Piazza del
Quirinale 🚌H, 40,
64, 70, 170 and many
routes along Via
del Tritone

Castor and Pollux and
their prancing horses
stand in the Piazza del
Quirinale. Over 5.5 m (18 ft)
high, these statues are
huge Roman copies of 5th-
century BC Greek originals.
They once stood at the
entrance to the nearby
Baths of Constantine.
Pope Sixtus V had them
restored and placed here
in 1588. They gave the
square its familiar name
of Monte Cavallo (horse hill).

The obelisk between
them was brought here in
1786 from the Mausoleum
of Augustus. In 1818 the
composition was completed
by the addition of a massive
granite basin, once a cattle
trough in the Forum.

Santi Apostoli

📍H5 🏛Piazza dei
Santi Apostoli 📞06-
699571 🚌H, 40, 64,
70, 170 and many other
routes to Piazza Venezia
🕐7am–noon & 4–
7pm daily

The 6th-century church
that was originally on
this site was rebuilt in
the 15th century by popes
Martin V Colonna and
Sixtus IV della Rovere,
whose oak-tree crest
decorates the capitals
of the late 15th-century
portico. Inside the portico
on the left is Canova's
1807 memorial to the
engraver Giovanni Volpato.
The church itself contains
a much larger monument
by Canova, his Tomb of
Clement XIV (1789).

The Baroque interior
by Francesco and Carlo
Fontana was completed
in 1714. Note the 3D effect
of Giovanni Odazzi's
painted *Rebel Angels*,
who really look as though
they are falling from the
sky. A huge 18th-century
altarpiece by Domenico
Muratori illustrates the
martyrdom of the Apostles
James and Philip, whose
tombs are in the crypt.

Palazzo del
Quirinale

📍J5 🏛Piazza del
Quirinale 🚌H, 40, 64,
70, 170 and many routes
along Via del Tritone
🕐Mid-Sep–late Jun:
9:30am–4pm Tue, Wed,
Fri–Sun 🕐Public hols
🌐palazzo.quirinale.it

By the 1500s, the
Vatican had a reputation
as an unhealthy location
because of the high inci-
dence of malaria, so Pope
Gregory XIII chose this
site as a papal summer
residence. Work began in
1573. Piazza del Quirinale
has buildings on three
sides, while the fourth
is open, with a splendid
view of the city. Many
great architects worked
on the palace.

After Rome became
the capital city of the new
united Italy in 1870, the
palace became the official
residence of the king, then,
in 1947, of the president
of the republic.

The immaculately
manicured gardens are
open to the public only
once a year, on Republic
Day (2 June).

←
Statue of Castor
and his horse
in the Piazza
del Quirinale

Santi Vincenzo e Anastasio

📍H4 🏛Vicolo dei Modelli 73 🚌52, 53, 61, 62, 63, 71, 80, 116, 119
🕐9am–8pm daily

Overlooking the Trevi Fountain is one of the most over-the-top Baroque façades in Rome. Its thickets of columns are crowned by the huge coat of arms of Cardinal Raimondo Mazzarino, better known as Cardinal Mazarin, chief minister of France, who commissioned Martino Longhi the Younger to build the church in 1650. The female bust above the door is of one of the cardinal's famous nieces, either Louis XIV's first love, Maria Mancini (1639–1715), or her younger sister, Ortensia.

In the apse, memorial plaques record the popes whose *praecordia* (a part of the heart) are enshrined behind the wall. This gruesome tradition was started at the end of the 16th century by Pope Sixtus V and continued until Pius X stopped it in the early 20th century.

San Marcello al Corso

📍H5 🏛Piazza di San Marcello 5 📞06-679 3910 🚌62, 63, 81, 85, 117, 119, 160, 492, 628
🕐7am–midnight Mon-Fri, 9am–midnight Sat & Sun

This church was originally one of the first places of Christian worship in Rome, which were known as *tituli*. A later Romanesque building on the site burned down in 1519, but it was rebuilt by Jacopo Sansovino with a single nave and many richly decorated private chapels on either side. The imposing travertine façade was designed by Carlo Fontana in late Baroque style. The third chapel on the right features fine frescoes of the Virgin Mary by Francesco Salviati. The decoration of the next chapel was interrupted by the Sack of Rome in 1527. Raphael's follower Perin del Vaga fled, leaving the ceiling frescoes to be completed by Daniele da Volterra and Pellegrino Tibaldi when peace returned to the city.

In the nave stands a splendid marble Venetian-style double tomb made by Sansovino around 1520; this is a memorial to Cardinal Giovanni Michiel (who was the victim of a Borgia poisoning in 1503) and his nephew, Bishop Antonio Orso.

Santa Maria in Trivio

⊙ H4 **⌂** Piazza dei Crociferi 49 **📞** 06-6789645 **🚌** 52, 53, 61, 62, 63, 71, 80, 116, 119 **🕐** 8am-noon & 4-8pm daily

It has been said that Italian architecture is one of façades, and nowhere is this clearer than in the 1570s façade of Santa Maria in Trivio, delightfully stuck on to the building behind it. Note the false windows. There is illusion inside too, particularly in the ceiling frescoes, which show scenes from the New Testament by Antonio Gherardi (1644–1702).

The name of this beautiful little church probably means "St Mary-at-the-meeting-of-three-roads".

The Baroque Santi Vincenzo e Anastasio, with the Trevi Fountain in the foreground

Sant'Andrea al Quirinale

⊙ J5 **⌂** Via del Quirinale 29 **📞** 06-487 4565 **🚌** 116, 117 and routes to Via del Tritone **🕐** 9am-noon & 3-6pm Tue-Sun

Known as the "Pearl of the Baroque" because of its beautiful roseate marble interior, Sant'Andrea was designed by Bernini and executed by his assistants between 1658 and 1670. It was built for the Jesuits, hence the many IHS emblems *(Iesus Hominum Salvator* – Jesus Saviour of Mankind).

The site for the church was wide but shallow, so Bernini pointed the long axis of his oval plan not towards the altar, but towards the sides; he then leads the eye round to the altar end. Here Bernini ordered works of art in various media which function not in isolation, but together. The crucified St Andrew (Sant'Andrea) of the altarpiece looks up at a stucco version of himself, who in turn ascends towards the lantern and the Holy Spirit.

The rooms of St Stanislas Kostka in the adjacent convent should not be missed. The quarters of the Jesuit novice, who died in 1568 at the age of 19, reflect not his own spartan taste, but the richer style of the 17th-century Jesuits.

The Polish saint has been brilliantly immortalized in marble by Pierre Legros (1666–1719).

Santi Domenico e Sisto

⊙ J6 **⌂** Largo Angelicum 1 **📞** 06-670 2201 **🚌** 40, 60, 64, 70, 71, 117, 170 **🕐** 3-6pm Sat

The church has a tall, slender Baroque façade rising above a steep flight of steps. This divides into two curving flights that sweep up to the terrace in front of the entrance. The pediment of the façade is crowned by eight flaming candlesticks.

The interior has a vaulted ceiling with a large fresco of *The Apotheosis of St Dominic* by Domenico Canuti (1620–84). The first chapel on the right was decorated by Bernini, who may also have designed the sculpture of Mary Magdalene meeting the risen Christ in the Garden of Gethsemane. This fine marble group was executed by Antonio Raggi (1649).

Above the altar is a 15th-century terracotta plaque of the Virgin and Child. On the left, over a side altar, is a large painting of the Madonna from the same period, attributed to Benozzo Gozzoli (1420–97), a pupil of Fra Angelico.

San Carlo alle Quattro Fontane

📍 J4 📌 Via del Quirinale 23 📞 06-488 3261 🚌 116, 117 and routes to Piazza Barberini Ⓜ Barberini 🕐 10am–1pm & 3–6pm Mon-Fri (mornings only Jul & Aug), 10am–1pm Sat & Sun

In 1634, the Trinitarians, a Spanish order whose role was to pay the ransom of Christian hostages to the Arabs, commissioned Borromini to design a church and convent at the Quattro Fontane crossroads. The church, so small it would fit inside one of the piers of St Peter's, is

The interior of the small church of San Carlo alle Quattro Fontane

also known as "San Carlino". Although dedicated to Carlo Borromeo, the 16th-century Milanese cardinal canonized in 1620, San Carlo is as much a monument to Borromini. Both the façade and interior employ bold curves that give light and life to a small, cramped site. The oval dome and tiny lantern are particularly ingenious. Finished in 1667, the façade is one of Borromini's last works.

There are further delights in the playful inverted shapes in the cloister and the stucco work in the refectory.

In a small room off the sacristy hangs a portrait of Borromini himself wearing the Trinitarian cross. Borromini committed suicide in 1667, and in the crypt a small curved chapel reserved for him remains empty.

Palazzo delle Esposizioni

📍 J5 📌 Via Nazionale 194 🚌 40, 60, 64, 70, 116T, 170 🕐 10am–8pm Tue-Sun (Fri & Sat: to 10:30pm) 🌐 palazzoesposizioni.it

This grandiose building, with wide steps, Corinthian columns and statues, was designed as an exhibition centre by the architect Pio Piacentini and built by the city of Rome in 1882 during the reign of Umberto I. The main entrance looks like a triumphal arch.

The restored palazzo still hosts high-profile exhibitions of modern and contemporary art that change every three to six months and include sculptures, paintings and photography. Live performances, films and lectures also take place here.

Piazza della Repubblica

📍 K4 🚌 36, 60, 61, 62, 64, 90, 170, 492, 646, 910 Ⓜ Repubblica

Romans often refer to the piazza by its old name, Piazza Esedra, so called

DRINK

Trimani Il Wine Bar

This celebrated enoteca offers plenty of wines by the glass and has been selling its wares to thirsty Romans since 1821. There's also a menu of dishes far above the usual wine-bar fare. Staff can advise on the perfect choice to pair with your meal.

📍 L3 📌 Via Cernaia 37B 🌐 trimani.com

because it follows the shape of an *exedra* (a semicircular recess) that was part of the Baths of Diocletian. The piazza was included in the great redevelopment undertaken when Rome became capital of a unified Italy. Under its sweeping 19th-century colonnades there were once elegant shops, but they have been ousted by banks, travel agencies and cafés.

In the middle of the piazza stands the Fontana delle Naiadi. Mario Rutelli's four naked bronze nymphs caused a scandal when unveiled in 1901. Each reclines on an aquatic creature symbolizing water in its various forms: a seahorse for the oceans, a water snake for rivers, a swan for lakes, and a curious frilled lizard for subterranean streams. The figure in the middle, added in 1911, is of the sea god Glaucus.

Sant'Agata dei Goti
📍 J5 🏛 Via Mazzarino 16 and Via Panisperna 29
📞 06-4893 0456 🚌 40, 60, 64, 70, 71, 117, 170
🕐 7am-1pm & 4-7pm daily

The Goths (*Goti*) who gave their name to this church occupied Rome in the 6th century AD. They were Aryan heretics who denied the divinity of Christ. The church was founded between AD 462 and 470, shortly before the main Gothic invasions, and the beautiful granite columns date from this period. The most delightful part of the church is the 18th-century courtyard built around a well.

EAT

Alle Carrette
This cheerful pizzeria serves up delicious thin-crust Roman-style pizzas. The tables outside on the cobbled street are in high demand in summer.

📍 J6 🏛 Via della Madonna dei Monti 95
📞 06-679 2270

L'Asino d'Oro
Italian dishes with a twist - such as wild boar with chocolate, or rabbit with pistachio - are what set apart this Monti favourite. Its cool, contemporary interior, lively atmosphere and inexpensive fixed lunchtime menu are further draws.

📍 J5 🏛 Via del Boschetto 73 📞 06-4891 3832

€€€

←
The once-controversial Fontana delle Naiadi in the Piazza della Repubblica

ESQUILINE

Central Rome's most multicultural quarter and one of the poorer areas of the city, the Esquiline's traffic-filled streets evoke gritty urban shabbiness interspersed with 19th-century elegance. Its most famous sights are the churches, whose interiors are mosaicked like jewellery boxes. This is the place for multi-ethnic dining options – take your pick of Eritrean, Chinese, Indian and Thai eateries. The huge, loud Nuovo Mercato Esquilino market represents all the different cultures here, and is full of the smells and colours of exotic spices and a vast array of international foods.

Coronation of the Virgin Mary mosaic in Santa Maria Maggiore
↓

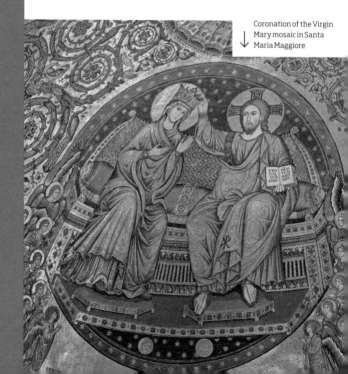

SANTA MARIA MAGGIORE

◉ L5 ⌂ Piazza di Santa Maria Maggiore ☎ 06-6988 6800 🚌 16, 70, 71, 714 🚋 14 Ⓜ Termini, Cavour ◷ 7am-6:45pm daily

Of all the great Roman basilicas, Santa Maria Maggiore has the most successful blend of different architectural styles. One of the four papal basilicas, it has a beautiful interior with sparkling mosaics.

This is the biggest of the 26 churches in Rome dedicated to the Virgin Mary. Originally built by Pope Liberius in the 4th century, Santa Maria Maggiore was renovated and improved upon by many popes over the centuries, although it still retains its early medieval structure. The colonnaded nave is part of the original 5th-century building. The Cosmatesque marble floor and delightful Romanesque bell tower, with its blue ceramic roundels, are medieval. The Renaissance saw a new coffered ceiling, and the Baroque gave the church twin domes and its imposing front and rear façades. The mosaics are Santa Maria's most famous feature and are some of the oldest in Rome. From the 5th century come the biblical scenes in the aisle and the spectacular mosaics on the triumphal arch. Medieval highlights include a 13th-century enthroned Christ in the loggia.

A series of wonderful apse mosaics of the Virgin by Jacopo Torriti (1295) is here.

Flaminio Ponzio designed this richly decorated chapel (1611) for Pope Paul V Borghese.

The Gothic Tomb of Cardinal Rodriguez (1299) contains Cosmatesque marblework.

This Sistine Chapel was built for Pope Sixtus V (1584–7) by Domenico Fontana and houses his tomb.

The gilded coffered ceiling, possibly by Giuliano da Sangallo, was a gift of Alexander VI Borgia at the end of the 15th century.

↑ Illustration showing the layout of the vast Santa Maria Maggiore basilica

←

Interior of Santa Pudenziana showing the splendid 4th-century apse mosaic

of its age are the ancient Corinthian columns dividing the nave and aisles. The most interesting interior features are a series of frescoed landscapes of the countryside around Rome *(campagna romana)* by the 17th-century French artist Gaspare Dughet, Poussin's brother-in-law, in the right aisle.

Santa Pudenziana

Q K5 **A** Via Urbana 160 **C** 06-481 4622 **■** 16, 75, 105, 714 **M** Cavour **C** 8:30am–noon & 3-6pm daily

Churches tend to be dedicated to existing saints, but this church, through a linguistic accident, created a brand new saint. In the 1st century AD a Roman senator called Pudens lived here, and is said to have allowed St Peter to lodge with him. In the 2nd century a bath house was built on this site and in the 4th century a church was established inside the baths, known as the *Ecclesia Pudentiana* (the church of Pudens). In time it was assumed that "Pudentiana" was a woman's name and a

EXPERIENCE MORE

San Martino ai Monti

Q L6 **A** Viale del Monte Oppio 28 **C** 06-478 4701 **■** 16, 714 **M** Cavour, Vittorio Emanuele **C** 7.30am–noon & 4-7pm daily

Christians have worshipped on the site of this church since the 3rd century, when they used to meet in the house of a man named Equitius. In the 4th century, after Constantine had legalized Christianity, Pope Sylvester I built a

church, one of the very few things he did during his pontificate. In fact he was so insignificant that in the 5th century a more exciting life was fabricated for him – which included tales of him converting Constantine and curing him of leprosy.

Pope Sylvester's church was replaced in about AD 500 by St Symmachus, rebuilt in the 9th century and then transformed completely in the 1630s. The only immediate signs life was created for her – she became the sister of Prassede and was credited with caring for Christian victims of persecution. In 1969 both saints were declared invalid.

The 19th-century façade of the church retains an 11th-century frieze depicting both Prassede and Pudenziana. The apse has a remarkable 4th-century mosaic influenced by Classical pagan art.

Santa Prassede

📍L5 🏛Via Santa Prassede 9A 📞06-488 2456 🚌16, 70, 71, 75, 714 Ⓜ Vittorio Emanuele 🕐7am–noon & 4-6:30pm daily (from 7:30am Sun; Aug: pm only)

The church was founded by Pope Paschal I in the 9th century, on the site of a 2nd-century oratory. Although the interior has been altered and rebuilt, the structure of the 9th-century church is visible. Its three aisles are separated by rows of granite columns. In the central nave, there is a round stone slab covering the well where, according to legend, Santa Prassede is said to have buried the remains of 2,000 martyrs.

Artists from Byzantium decorated the church with glittering, jewel-coloured mosaics. Those in the apse and choir depict stylized white-robed elders, the haloed elect looking down from the gold and blue walls of heaven, spindly legged lambs, feather-mop palm trees and bright-red poppies. In the apse, Santa Prassede and Santa Pudenziana stand on either side of Christ, with the fatherly arms of St Paul and St Peter on their shoulders. Beautiful mosaics of saints, the Virgin and Christ, and the Apostles also cover the walls and vault of the Chapel of St Zeno, built as a mausoleum for Pope Paschal's mother, Theodora. Part of a column brought back from Jerusalem, allegedly the one to which Christ was bound and flogged, also stands here.

Arch of Gallienus

📍L6 🏛Via Carlo Alberto 🚌16, 71, 714 Ⓜ Vittorio Emanuele

Squashed between two buildings just off Via Carlo Alberto is the central arch of an originally three-arched gate erected in memory of Emperor Gallienus, who was assassinated by his Illyrian officers in AD 262. It was built on the site of the old Esquiline Gate in the Servian Wall, parts of which are visible nearby.

EAT

Trattoria Monti

This cosy, ever-popular neighbourhood trattoria specializes in the cuisine of the Marche region, with hearty pasta dishes and superb beef, lamb and rabbit mains. It's on the small side and hugely popular, so booking is essential.

📍L6 🏛Via di San Vito 13 📞06-446 6573

 €€€

Palazzo del Freddo di Giovanni Fassi

This time-warp gelateria is worth visiting for its 1950s ice-cream parlour decor alone - and the gelato's not bad either, with all the classics, as well as more unusual flavours such as rose and cardamom.

📍M6 🏛Via Principe Eugenio 65 🌐gelateriafassi.com

 €€€

San Pietro in Vincoli

K6 ⌂ Piazza di San Pietro in Vincoli 4A
📞 06-9784 4950 🚌 75, 117 Ⓜ Cavour, Colosseo
🕐 8am-12.30pm & 3-7pm (Oct-Mar: until 6pm) daily

According to tradition, the two chains (*vincoli*) used to shackle St Peter while he was being held in the depths of the Mamertine Prison were subsequently taken to Constantinople. In the 5th century, Empress Eudoxia deposited one in a church there and sent the other to her daughter Eudoxia in Rome. She in turn gave hers to Pope Leo I, who had this church built to house it. Some years later the second chain was brought to Rome, where it linked miraculously with its partner.

The chains are still here, displayed below the high altar, but the church is now best known for Michelangelo's *Tomb of Pope Julius II*. When it was commissioned in 1505, Michelangelo spent eight months searching for perfect blocks of marble at Carrara in Tuscany, but Pope Julius became more interested in the building of a new St Peter's and the project was laid aside. After the pope's death in 1513, Michelangelo resumed work on the tomb, but had only finished the statues of *Moses* and *The Dying Slaves* when Pope Paul III persuaded him to start work on the Sistine Chapel's *Last Judgment*. Michelangelo had planned a vast monument with over 40 statues, but the tomb that was built – mainly by his pupils – is simply a façade with six niches for statues. *The Dying Slaves* are in Paris and Florence, but the tremendous bearded *Moses* is here, nearly 2.5 m (8 feet)in height, with his huge muscular arms and intense expression.

Piazza Vittorio Emanuele II

M6 🚌 4, 9, 71 🚊 5, 14
Ⓜ Vittorio Emanuele

Rome's largest square, Piazza Vittorio, as it is called for short, was once one of the city's main open-air food markets. The market moved around the corner to covered premises in 2001 and is now called Nuovo Mercato Esquilino. The arcaded square was built as part of the urban development that was undertaken following the unification of Italy in 1861. It was named after Italy's first king, but there is nothing regal about its appearance today. The garden area in the centre of the square contains a number of mysterious ruins, including a large mound, part of a Roman fountain from the 3rd century AD and the Porta Magica, a curious 17th-century doorway inscribed with alchemical signs and formulae, which belonged to a marquis whose home was often visited by alchemists and magicians.

Santa Bibiana

Q M6 **A** Via Giovanni
Giolitti 154 **C** 06-446 5235
🚌 71 **🚋** 5, 14 **M** Vittorio
Emanuele **🕐** 7:30-10am
& 4:30-7:30pm Mon-Sat,
7:30am-12:30pm & 4:30-
7:30pm Sun

The deceptively simple
façade of Santa Bibiana was
Bernini's first foray into architecture. It is a clean, economic
design with superimposed
pilasters and deeply shad-
owed archways. The church
itself was built on the site
of the palace belonging
to Bibiana's family. This is
where the saint was buried
after being flogged to death
with leaded cords during
the brief persecution of the
Christians in the reign of
Julian the Apostate (361-3).
Just inside the church is a
small column against which
Bibiana is said to have been
whipped. Her remains, along
with those of her mother
Dafrosa and her sister
Demetria, who also suf-
fered martyrdom, are
preserved in an alabaster
urn below the altar.

In a niche above the altar
stands a statue of Santa
Bibiana by Bernini – the first
fully clothed figure he ever
sculpted. He depicts her
standing beside a column,
holding the cords with

←

The Porta Magica in Piazza
Vittorio Emanuele II

which she was whipped,
apparently on the verge
of a deadly swoon.

Domus Aurea

Q K6 **A** Viale della
Domus Aurea **🚌** 85, 87,
117, 186, 810, 850 **🚋** 3
M Colosseo **🕐** For guided
tours (on weekends only)
book online; virtual tours
are available online also
W coopculture.it

After allegedly setting
fire to Rome in AD 64,
Nero decided to build
himself an outrageous
new palace. The Domus
Aurea (sometimes called
Nero's Golden House)
occupied part of the
Palatine and most of the
Celian and Esquiline hills –
an area approximately
25 times the size of the
Colosseum. The vestibule
on the Palatine side of
the complex contained a
colossal gilded statue of
Nero. There was an artificial
lake, with gardens and
woods where imported
wild beasts were allowed
to roam free. According
to Suetonius in his *Life of
Nero*, the Domus Aurea's
walls were adorned with
gold and mother-of-pearl,
rooms had ceilings that
showered guests with
flowers or perfumes, the
dining hall rotated and
the baths were fed with
both sulphurous water
and sea water.

→

A bust of Emperor
Nero at the park
entrance to the
Domus Aurea

Tacitus
described
Nero's
debauched garden parties,
with banquets served on
barges and lakeside brothels
serviced by aristocratic
women. Since Nero killed
himself in AD 68, however,
he did not have long to
enjoy his new home.

Nero's successors, anxious
to distance themselves
from the monster-emperor,
did their utmost to erase
all traces of the palace.
Vespasian drained the lake
and built the Colosseum in
its place, Titus and Trajan
each erected a complex of
baths over the palace, and
Hadrian placed the Temple
of Venus and Rome over
the vestibule.

Rooms from one wing
of the palace have survived,
buried beneath the ruins
of the Baths of Trajan on
the Oppian Hill. Excavations
have revealed large fres-
coes and mosaics that are
thought to be a panorama
of Rome from a bird's-
eye perspective.

Visitors are advised
to bring a jacket as the
temperature inside
the building is around
10° C (50° F).

LATERAN

Traditionally a working-class area, the Lateran retains an unpretentious feel, its left-wing traditions and loyalties still evident in the huge free May Day concert organized every year by the trades unions in the central large Piazza di San Giovanni. Modern avenues open out onto beautiful churches – the Lateran is the site of Rome's oldest basilica, San Giovanni. The area is also home to the huge Via Sannio clothes and shoes market.

Concert in Piazza di San Giovanni, part of the annual 1st May festivities

SAN GIOVANNI IN LATERANO

📍M8 🏛Piazza di San Giovanni in Laterano 4 📞06-6988 6433 🚌16, 81, 85, 87, 186, 650, 850 🚊3 Ⓜ San Giovanni 🕐Cathedral: 7am–6:30pm; Cloister: 9am–6pm; Museum: 10am–5:30pm; Baptistry: 9am–12:30pm & 4–6:30pm

In the 4th century, the Laterani family were disgraced and their land taken by Emperor Constantine to build Rome's first Christian basilica, San Giovanni in Laterano. This is the cathedral of Rome's bishopric.

Today's church retains the original shape, but has been destroyed by fire twice and rebuilt several times. Borromini undertook the last major rebuild of the interior in 1646, and the main façade is an 18th-century addition. Before the pope's move to Avignon in 1309, the adjoining Lateran Palace was the official papal residence, and until 1870 all popes were crowned in the church. This is the city's main cathedral, and the seat of the Bishop of Rome, the pope, who celebrates Maundy Thursday Mass here. This is also where the pope attends the annual blessing of the people. The church has the world's first baptistry – its octagonal shape formed the model for all those to come.

TRIAL OF A CORPSE

Fear of rival factions led the early popes to extraordinary lengths. At the Lateran Palace in 897 Pope Stephen VI tried the corpse of his predecessor, Formosus, for disloyalty to the Church. The corpse was found guilty, its right hand was mutilated and it was thrown into the Tiber.

→

Papal altar with the Gothic baldacchino, decorated with frescoes

Courtyard of the San Clemente basilica; the 12th-century apse mosaic of the *Triumph of the Cross (inset)*

SAN CLEMENTE

📍 K7 🏛 Via di San Giovanni in Laterano 🚌 85, 87, 117, 186, 810, 850
🚊 3 Ⓜ Colosseo 🕐 9am–12:30pm & 3–6pm Mon–Sat, noon–6pm Sun
🌐 basilicasanclemente.com

San Clemente gives visitors a chance to travel back through three layers of history, providing an insight into how buildings were modified over the years.

At street level, the present-day basilica dates to the 12th century. It features medieval mosaics and Renaissance frescoes, notably those depicting St Catherine of Alexandria by the 15th-century Florentine artist Masolino da Panicale. Underneath lies a 4th-century church built to honour San Clemente, the fourth pope, who was exiled to the Crimea and martyred by being tied to an anchor and drowned. His life is illustrated in some of the frescoes.

This 4th-century church was built over a temple dedicated to the cult of Mithras, which in turn was built inside a 1st-century AD aristocratic house. The site was taken over in the 17th century by Irish Dominicans, who still continue the excavations begun by Father Mullooly in 1857.

THE CULT OF MITHRAS

In 3rd-century Rome the all-male cult of Mithras rivalled Christianity. Followers believed that Mithras had brought life to the world by spilling the blood of a bull and that faith in Mithras guaranteed salvation. Would-be cult members underwent initiation ceremonies, including trials by ice, fire, hunger and thirst. Ritual banquets were held in the triclinium, a room with stone benches on either side of an altar.

EXPERIENCE MORE

Museum of Musical Instruments

⊕ P7 **⌂** Piazza di Santa Croce in Gerusalemme 9A **🚌** 16, 81, 649, 810 **🚊** 3 **⊕** 9am-7pm Tue–Sun **🖥** museostrument imusicali.beniculturali.it

One of Rome's lesser-known museums, the Museum of Musical Instruments stands on the site of the Sessorianum, the great Imperial villa belonging to Empress St Helena, later included in the Aurelian Wall. It houses a collection of more than 3,000 outstanding musical instruments from all over the world, including instruments typical of the various regions of Italy, and wind, string and percussion instruments of all ages (including ancient Egyptian, Greek and Roman). There are also sections dedicated to church and military music. The greater part of the collection comprises Baroque instruments: be sure to see the gorgeous Barberini harp (dating to 1605–20), which is remarkably well-preserved, on the first floor in Room 13. There are also fine examples of spinets, harpsichords and clavichords, and one of the first pianos ever made, dating from 1722.

Santo Stefano Rotondo

⊕ K8 **⌂** Via di Santo Stefano Rotondo 7 **☎** 06-421199 **🚌** 81, 117, 673 **⊕** 10am–1pm & 3:30–6:30pm (2:30–5:30pm winter) daily **⊗** Three weeks in Aug

One of Rome's earliest Christian churches, Santo Stefano Rotondo was built between 468 and 483. It has an unusual circular plan with four chapels in the shape of a cross. It is lit by 22 high windows, a few of them restored or blocked by restorations carried out under Pope Nicholas V (reigned 1447–55), who consulted the Florentine architect Leon Battista Alberti.

The archway in the centre may have been added during this period. In the 16th century the church walls were frescoed by Niccolò Pomaranciowith particularly gruesome illustrations of the martyrdom of innumerable saints. Some of the medieval decor remains: in the first chapel to the left of the entrance is a 7th-century mosaic of Christ with San Primo and San Feliciano.

Museo Storico della Liberazione di Roma

⊕ M7 **⌂** Via Tasso 145 **☎** 06-700 3866 **Ⓜ** Manzoni, San Giovanni **🚊** 3 **⊕** 9am–1:15pm & 2:15–8pm daily **⊗** Aug

This museum, dedicated to the resistance to the Nazi occupation of Rome during World War II, is housed in the ex-prison of the Gestapo. The makeshift cells with bloodstained walls make a strong impact.

→ Unusual circular plan of the Santo Stefano Rotondo

Santa Croce in Gerusalemme

Q P7 **A** Piazza di Santa Croce in Gerusalemme 12
🚌 16, 81, 649, 810
🚊 3 **🕐** 7am–12:45pm & 3:30–7:30pm daily
W santacroceroma.it

Emperor Constantine's mother St Helena founded this church in AD 320 in the grounds of her private palace. Although the church stood at the edge of the city, the relics of the Crucifixion that St Helena had brought back from Jerusalem made it a centre of pilgrimage. Most important were the pieces of Christ's Cross (*croce* means "cross") and part of Pontius Pilate's inscription in Latin, Hebrew and Greek: "Jesus of Nazareth King of the Jews".

In the crypt is a Roman statue of Juno, found at Ostia, transformed into a statue of St Helena by replacing the head and arms.

The 15th-century apse fresco shows the medieval legends that arose around the Cross. Helena is shown holding over a dead youth and restoring him to life. Another episode shows its recovery from the Persians by the Byzantine Emperor Heraclitus after a bloody battle. In the centre of the apse is a tomb by Jacopo Sansovino made for Cardinal Quiñones, Emperor Charles V's confessor (died 1540).

→

The 28 steps of the Scala Santa, with devotees kneeling and praying

Scala Santa and Sancta Sanctorum

Q M7 **A** Piazza di San Giovanni in Laterano 14
📞 06-772 6641 **🚌** 16, 81, 85, 87, 186 and other routes to Piazza di San Giovanni in Laterano
🚊 3 **Ⓜ** San Giovanni
🕐 6:30am–6:30pm Mon–Sat, 7am–7pm Sun & hols

On the east side of Piazza di San Giovanni in Laterano, a building by Domenico Fontana (1589) houses two surviving parts of the old Lateran Palace. One is the Sancta Sanctorum, the other the holy staircase, the Scala Santa. The 28 steps, said to be those that Christ ascended in Pontius Pilate's house during his trial, are said to have been brought from Jerusalem by St Helena, the mother of Constantine. This belief, however, cannot be traced back any earlier than the 7th century.

The steps were moved to their present site by Pope Sixtus V (reigned 1585–90) when the old Lateran Palace was destroyed. No foot may touch the holy steps, so they are covered by wooden boards. They may only be climbed by the faithful on their knees, especially on Good Friday.

In the vestibule there are various 19th-century sculptures including an *Ecce Homo* by Giosuè Meli (1874).

The Scala Santa and two side stairways lead to the Chapel of St Lawrence or Sancta Sanctorum (Holy of Holies), built by Pope Nicholas III in 1278. Decorated with fine Cosmatesque marble-work, the chapel contains many important relics, the most precious being an image of Jesus – the *Acheiropoeton* or "picture painted without hands", said to be the work of St Luke, with the help of an angel. It was taken on procession in medieval times to ward off plagues.

On the walls and in the vault, restoration work has revealed 13th-century frescoes which for 500 years had been covered by later paintings.

Aqueduct of Nero and the Freedmen's Tombs

Q N6 **Intersection of Via Statilia and Via di Santa Croce in Gerusalemme** 🚌 105, 649 🚋 3, 5, 14, 19 **By appt (call 06-0608)**

The aqueduct was built by Nero in the 1st century AD as an extension of the Aqua Claudia to supply Nero's Golden House. Partly incorporated into later buildings, the arches make their way via the Lateran to the Celian Hill. Along the first section of the aqueduct, in Via Statilia, is a small tomb in the shape of a house, dating from the 1st century BC, bearing the names and likenesses of a group of slaves freed by the Statilii, the family of Claudius's notorious wife Messalina.

Porta Asinaria

Q M8 **Between Piazza di Porta San Giovanni and Piazzale Appio** 🚌 16, 81, 85, 87 🚋 3 🚇 San Giovanni

The Porta Asinaria (Gate of the Donkeys) is one of the minor gateways built between 270 and 273 in the Aurelian Wall. Twin circular towers were added and a small enclosure was built around the entrance; the remains are still visible. From outside the walls you can see the gate's white travertine façade and two rows of small windows, giving light

to two corridors built into the wall above the gateway. In AD 546 treacherous barbarian soldiers serving in the Roman army opened this gate to the hordes of the Goth Totila, who mercilessly looted the city. In 1084 the Holy Roman Emperor Henry IV entered Rome via Porta Asinaria with the antipope Guibert to oust Pope Gregory VII. The gate was badly damaged in the conflicts that followed. The area close to the gate in the Via Sannio is the home of a large flea market held from 8am to 1pm Monday to Friday and 8am until 6pm on Saturday.

Porta Maggiore

Q N7 **Piazza di Porta Maggiore** 🚌 105 🚋 3, 5, 14, 19

Originally the arches of Porta Maggiore were not part of the city wall, but part of an aqueduct built by the Emperor Claudius in AD 52. They carried the water of the Aqua Claudia over the Via Labicana and Via Prenestina, two of ancient Rome's main south-bound roads. You can still see the original roadway beneath the gate. In the large slabs of basalt – a hard volcanic rock used in all old Roman roads – note the great ruts created by centuries of cartwheel traffic. On top of the arches separate conduits carried the water of two aqueducts: the Aqua Claudia,

and its offshoot, the Aqueduct of Nero. They bear inscriptions from the time of the Emperor Claudius and also from the reigns of Vespasian and Titus. In all, six aqueducts from different water sources entered the city at Porta Maggiore. The Aqua Claudia was 68 km (43 miles) long, with over 15 km (9 miles) above ground. Its majestic arches are a notable feature of the Roman countryside, and a popular mineral water bears its name. One stretch of the Aqua Claudia had its arches bricked up when it was incorporated into the 3rd-century Aurelian Wall.

CARACALLA

Largely undeveloped except for an immense military hospital and a handful of beguiling churches, the Celian Hill rises, green and tranquil, from the busy thoroughfares that now cut along the valleys at its foot. It's a lovely place to stroll from one little church to the next along quiet roads. The Villa Celimontana park, at its heart, is perfect for a picnic, while anyone who really loves to walk can carry right on beyond the ancient city walls to the Via Appia Antica.

↓ Ancient ruins in the grounds of Villa Celimontana

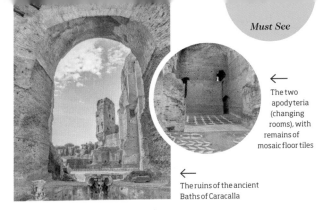

The two apodyteria (changing rooms), with remains of mosaic floor tiles ←

The ruins of the ancient Baths of Caracalla ←

BATHS OF CARACALLA

📍K9 🏠Viale delle Terme di Caracalla 52 🚌160, 628 🚋3 Ⓜ Circo Massimo 🕐9am–2pm Mon, 9am–approximately 1 hour before sunset Tue–Sun 🌐isromantique.it

Completed by Emperor Caracalla in AD 217, the baths functioned for around 300 years until the acqueducts feeding them were sabotaged by invading Goths. This is one of the most enjoyable and best preserved ancient sites in the city.

Over 1,600 bathers at a time could enjoy the facilities, which included not only baths and gymnasia but gardens, shops selling food and drink, a library, art galleries, lecture rooms and, inevitably doing a roaring trade, a host of pimps, gigolos and prostitutes. In summer the Baths of Caracalla now hosts a hugely popular festival of opera and ballet in the caldarium.

Inside the Baths

The *apodyterium* (changing room) was where people removed their clothes before bathing. They would then head to a hot steam room *(laconia)*, designed like Turkish baths, to induce sweat. This was followed by a hot bath in a bronze tub *(caldarium)*. The skin was then scraped to remove dead skin and dirt. Bathers then headed into the luke-warm waters of the *tepidarium*, followed by a plunge into the freezing-cold indoor pool, the *frigidarium*. The final stage was a swim in the outdoor pool *(natatio)*.

INSIDER TIP
Virtual Reality Tours

The Baths of Caracalla is the first archaeological site in Italy to be brought to life with virtual reality goggles. Reconstructions of the entire site are viewable in 3D through the headsets with audio commentary.

←
The basilica of Santi Giovanni e Paolo on the Celian Hill

EXPERIENCE MORE

Santi Giovanni e Paolo

Q K8 **A** Piazza Santi Giovanni e Paolo 13 **C** 06-772711 **B** 75, 81, 117, 673 **B** 3 **M** Colosseo or Circo Massimo **O** 8:30am–noon & 3:30–6pm daily

Santi Giovanni e Paolo is dedicated to two martyred Roman officers whose house originally stood on this site. Giovanni (John) and Paolo (Paul) had served the first Christian emperor, Constantine. When they were later called to arms by the pagan emperor Julian the Apostate, they refused and were beheaded and buried in secret in their own house in AD 362.

Built towards the end of the 4th century, the church retains many elements of its original structure. The Ionic portico dates from the 12th century, and the apse and bell tower were added by Nicholas Breakspeare, the only English pope, who reigned as Adrian IV (1154–9). The base of the impressive 13th-century Romanesque bell tower was part of the Temple of Claudius that stood on this site. The interior, which was remodelled in 1718, has granite piers and columns. A tomb slab in the nave marks the burial place of the martyrs, whose relics are preserved in an urn under the high altar. In a tiny room near the altar, a magnificent 13th-century fresco depicts the figure of Christ flanked by his Apostles (to see it, ask the sacristan who will be able to unlock the door).

Excavations carried out beneath the church have revealed two 2nd- and 3rd-century Roman houses, the Case Romane del Celio, that were used as a Christian burial place. Well worth a visit, the Roman houses, which include 20 rooms and a labyrinth of corridors, have beautifully restored pagan and Christian frescoes. The walls are painted to resemble precious marble. The arches that are found to the left of the church were originally part of a 3rd-century street of shops.

Arch of Dolabella

Q K8 **A** Via di San Paolo della Croce **B** 81, 117, 673 **B** 3 **M** Colosseo

The arch was built in AD 10 by consuls Caius Junius Silanus and Cornelius Dolabella, possibly on the site of one of the old Servian Wall's gateways. It was made of travertine blocks and later used to support Nero's extension of the Claudian aqueduct, built to supply the Imperial Palace on the Palatine Hill.

Santa Maria in Domnica

♀K8 **🏠**Piazza della Navicella 12 **☎**06-7720 2685 **🚌**81,117,673 **🚋**3 **Ⓜ**Colosseo **◷**For Mass only construction work is undertaken on Metro C; call for latest information

The church overlooks the Piazza della Navicella (little boat) and takes its name from the 16th-century fountain. Dating from the 7th century, the church was probably built on the site of an ancient Roman firemen's barracks, which later became a meeting place for Christians. In the 16th century Pope Leo X added the portico and the coffered ceiling.

In the apse behind the modern altar is a superb 9th-century mosaic commissioned by Pope Paschal I. Wearing the square halo of the living, the pope appears at the feet of the Virgin and Child. The Virgin, surrounded by a throng of angels, holds a handkerchief like a fashionable lady at a Byzantine court.

Villa Celimontana

♀K8 **🏠**Piazza della Navicella **🚌**81,117,673 Park: **◷**7am–dusk daily

The Dukes of Mattei bought this land in 1553 and transformed the vineyards that covered the hillside into a formal garden. As well as palms and other exotic trees, the garden has its own Egyptian obelisk. Villa Mattei, built in the 1580s and now known as Villa Celimontana, houses the Italian Geographical Society.

The Mattei family used to open the park to the public on the day of the Visit of the Seven Churches, an annual event instituted by San Filippo Neri in 1552. Starting from the Chiesa Nuova, Romans went on foot to the city's seven major churches and, on reaching Villa Mattei, were given bread, wine, salami, cheese, an egg and two apples. The pine-shaded park, now owned by the city of Rome, makes an ideal place for a picnic and has a playground with swings.

San Gregorio Magno

♀J8 **🏠**Piazza di San Gregorio 1 **☎**06-700 8227 **🚌**75, 81, 117, 673 **🚋**3 **Ⓜ**Circo Massimo **◷**9am–1pm & 3:30–7pm daily

Historically, this church has links with England, for it was from here that St Augustine was sent on his mission to convert England to Christianity. The church was founded in AD 575 by San Gregorio Magno (St Gregory the Great), who turned his family home on this site into a monastery. It was rebuilt in medieval times and restored in 1629–33 by Giovanni Battista Soria. The church is reached via steps from the street.

The forecourt contains some interesting tombs. To the left is that of Sir Edward Carne, who came to Rome several times between 1529 and 1533 as King Henry VIII's envoy to gain the pope's consent to the annulment of Henry's marriage to Catherine of Aragon.

The interior, remodelled by Francesco Ferrari in the mid-18th century, is Baroque, apart from the fine mosaic floor and some ancient columns. At the end of the right aisle is the chapel of St Gregory. Leading off it, another small chapel, believed to have been the saint's own cell, houses his episcopal throne – a Roman chair of sculpted marble. The Salviati Chapel, on the left, contains a picture of the Virgin said to have spoken to St Gregory.

Outside, amid the cypresses to the left of the church, stand three small chapels, dedicated to St Andrew, St Barbara and St Sylvia (Gregory the Great's mother). The chapels contain frescoes by Domenichino and Guido Reni.

San Sisto Vecchio

⚐K9 ⌂Piazzale Numa Pompilio 8 ☎06-7720 5174 🚌160, 628, 671, 714 ⏰9-11am & 3-5:30pm daily

This small church is of great historical interest, as it was granted to St Dominic in 1219 by Pope Honorius III. The founder of the Dominican order soon moved his own head-quarters to Santa Sabina, San Sisto becoming the first home of the order of Dominican nuns, who still occupy the monastery. The church, with its 13th-century bell tower and frescoes, is also a popular place for weddings.

San Giovanni a Porta Latina

⚐L10 ⌂Via di San Giovanni a Porta Latina ☎06-7047 5938 🚌218, 360, 628 ⏰7:30am-12:30pm & 3-7pm daily

The church of St John at the Latin Gate, founded in the 5th century, rebuilt in 720 and restored in 1191, is one of the most pictur-esque of the old Roman churches. Classical columns support the medieval por-tico, and the 12th-century bell tower is superb. A tall cedar tree shades an ancient well standing in the fore-court. The interior has been restored, but it preserves the rare simplicity of its early origins, with ancient columns of varying styles lining the aisles. Traces of early medieval frescoes can still be seen within the church. The beautiful 12th-century frescoes created by several different artists under the direction of one master, show 46 different biblical scenes, from both the Old and New Testaments and are among the finest of their kind in Rome.

San Giovanni in Oleo

⚐L10 ⌂Via di Porta Latina ☎06-7740 0032 🚌628 ⏰Ask at San Giovanni a Porta Latina

The name of this charming octagonal Renaissance chapel or oratory means "St John in Oil". The tiny build-ing marks the spot where, according to legend, St John was boiled in oil – and came out unscathed, or even refreshed. An earlier chapel is said to have existed on the site; the present one was built in the early 16th cen-tury. The design has been attributed to Baldassare Peruzzi or Antonio da Sangallo the Younger. In the mid-17th century it was restored by Borromini, who altered the roof, crowning it with a cross supported by a sphere decorated with roses. Borromini also added a terracotta frieze of roses and palm leaves. The wall paintings inside the chapel include one of St John in a cauldron of boiling oil.

Museo delle Mura

⚐L10 ⌂Via di Porta San Sebastiano 18 🚌218, 360 ⏰9am-2pm Tue-Sun (last adm: 30 mins before closing) ⏰1 Jan, 1 May, 25 Dec 🌐museodelle muraroma.it

Most of the Aurelian Wall, begun by the Emperor

Classical columns
inside the San Giovanni
a Porta Latina

Aurelian (AD 270–75) and
completed by his successor
Probus (AD 276–82), has
survived. Aurelian ordered
its construction as a
defence against Germanic
tribes, whose raids were
penetrating deeper and
deeper into Italy. Some
18 km (11 miles) round,
with 18 gates and 381
towers, the wall took in
all the seven hills of Rome.
It was raised to almost
twice its original height
by Maxentius (AD 306–12).

The wall was Rome's
main defence until 1870,
when it was breached
by Italian artillery just by
Porta Pia, close to today's
British Embassy. Many
of the gates are still in
use, and although the
city has spread, most of
its noteworthy historical
and cultural sights still
lie within the wall.

Porta San Sebastiano,
the gate leading to the Via
Appia Antica, is the largest and best-preserved
gateway in the Aurelian
Wall. It was rebuilt by
Emperor Honorius in the
5th century AD. Originally
the Porta Appia, in Christian
times it gradually became
known as the Porta San
Sebastiano, because the

Via Appia led to the basilica
and catacombs of San
Sebastiano, which were
popular places of pilgrimage.

It was at this gate that
the last triumphal procession to enter the city by the
Appian Way was received in
state – that of Marcantonio
Colonna after the victory
of Lepanto over the Turkish
fleet in 1571. Today the
gate's towers house a free
museum with prints and
models showing the wall's
history. From here you can
take a short walk along one
of the best-preserved
stretches of the wall.

Santi Nereo e Achilleo

📍 K9 🏠 Via delle Terme
di Caracalla 28 📞 06-687
3124 🚌 160, 628, 671,
714 🕐 noon–12:30pm Sun
(for half an hour only)

According to legend,
St Peter, after escaping
from prison, was fleeing
the city when he lost a
bandage from his wounds.
The original church was
founded here in the 4th
century on the spot where
the bandage fell, but it was
later re-dedicated to the
1st-century AD martyrs
St Nereus and St Achilleus.

Restored at the end
of the 16th century, the
church has retained many
medieval features, including several fine 9th-century
mosaics on the triumphal

arch. A magnificent pulpit
rests on an enormous
porphyry pedestal which
was found nearby in the
Baths of Caracalla. The
walls of the side aisles
are decorated with grisly
16th-century frescoes
by Niccolò Pomarancio,
showing in clinical detail
how each of the Apostles
was martyred.

Columbarium of Pomponius Hylas

📍 L10 🏠 Via di Porta
Latina 10 📞 06-0608
🚌 218, 360, 628
🕐 For guided tours
only; phone ahead

Known as a columbarium
because it resembles a
dovecote (columba is the
Latin word for "dove"),
this kind of vaulted tomb
was usually built by rich
Romans to house the
cremated remains of
their freedmen.

Many similar tombs
have been uncovered in
this part of Rome, which
up until the 3rd century AD
lay outside the city wall.
This one dates from the
1st century AD. An inscription states that it is the
tomb of Pomponius Hylas
and his wife, Pomponia
Vitalinis. Above her name
is a "V" which indicates
that she was still living
when the inscription
was made.

AVENTINE

Rising above the Tiber River to the southwest of the Palatine, the twin-peaked Aventine Hill is a lush, leafy residential area with a handful of early Christian churches scattered among its secluded villas, gardens and convents. Although in the centre of Rome, it is remarkably peaceful, and for once the sound of birdsong is louder than the roar of traffic. On the far side of the hill, Testaccio, a working-class neighbourhood defined by the huge market at its heart, is one of Rome's trendiest areas and the best place in the city for anyone seriously interested in food.

Grass esplanade of the Circus Maximus, from where there is a good ↓ view of the Palatine Hill

EXPERIENCE

San Giorgio in Velabro

⊙H7 **⌂**Via del Velabro 19 **☎**06-6979 7536 **🚌**23, 44, 81, 160, 170, 280, 628, 715, 716, 780 **◷**10am-12:30pm & 4-6:15pm Tue, Fri & Sat

In the hollow of the street named after the Velabrum, the swamp where Romulus and Remus are said to have been found by the she-wolf, is a small church dedicated to St George, whose bones lie under the altar.

The 7th-century basilica has suffered over time from floods. Careful restoration has, however, returned it to its original appearance. A double row of granite and marble columns (taken from ancient Roman temples) divides the triple nave. The austerity of the grey interior is relieved by golden frescoes in the apse (attributed to Pietro Cavallini, 1295). The façade and the bell tower date from the 1100s.

Arch of Janus

⊙H7 **⌂**Via del Velabro **🚌**23, 44, 63, 81, 160, 170, 280, 628, 715, 716, 780

Probably dating from the reign of Constantine, this imposing four-faced marble arch stood at the crossroads on the edge of the Forum Boarium, near the ancient docks. Merchants did business in its shade. On the keystones above the four arches you can see small figures of the goddesses Roma, Juno, Ceres and Minerva. In medieval times the arch formed the base of a tower fortress. It was finally restored to its original shape in 1827.

Santa Maria in Cosmedin

⊙H7 **⌂**Piazza della Bocca della Verità 18 **☎**06-678 7759 **🚌**23, 44, 81, 160, 170, 280, 628, 715, 716 **◷**9:30am-6pm daily (winter: to 5pm); gates shut 10 mins before closing

This beautiful unadorned church was built in the 6th century on the site of the ancient city's food market. The elegant Romanesque bell tower and portico were added during the 12th century. In the 19th century a Baroque façade was removed and the church restored to its original simplicity. It contains many fine examples of Cosmati work, in particular the mosaic pavement, the raised choir, the bishop's throne and the canopy over the main altar. Set into the wall of the portico is the Bocca della Verità (Mouth of Truth). This may have been a drain cover, dating back to before the 4th century BC. Medieval tradition had it that the formidable jaws would snap shut over the hand of those who told lies – a useful trick for testing the faithfulness of spouses.

Casa dei Crescenzi

⊙H7 **⌂**Via Luigi Petroselli **🚌**23, 44, 63, 81, 160, 170, 280, 628, 715, 716, 780

Studded with archaeological fragments, this house is what remains of an 11th-century tower fortress. The Crescenzi family built it to keep an eye on the docks and bridge where they collected a toll. It is only viewable from outside.

San Teodoro

⊙H7 **⌂**Via di San Teodoro 7 **☎**06-678 6624 **🚌**23, 44, 81, 160, 170, 280, 628, 715, 716 **◷**9:30am-12:30pm Sun-Fri

This small, round 6th-century church at the foot of the Palatine has breathtaking 6th-century mosaics in the apse, and a Florentine cupola dating from 1454. The fetching outer courtyard was designed by Carlo Fontana in 1705.

←
The 13th-century
Romanesque bell tower
of Santi Bonifacio e Alessio

Santi Bonifacio e Alessio

📍G8 🏛️Piazza di Sant'Alessio 23 📞06-574 3446 🚌23, 280, 716 Ⓜ️Circo Massimo ⏰For special events only

The church is dedicated to two early Christian martyrs, whose remains lie under the main altar. Legend has it that Alessio, son of a rich senator living on the site, fled east to avoid an impending marriage and became a pilgrim. Returning home after many years, he died as a servant, unrecognized, under the stairs of the family entrance hall, clutching the manuscript of his story for posterity. The original 5th-century church has undergone many changes over time. Noteworthy are the 18th-century façade with its five arches, the restored Cosmati doorway and pavement, and the magnificent Romanesque five-storey bell tower (1217).

An 18th-century Baroque chapel by Andrea Bergondi houses part of the staircase.

Il Mattatoio

📍F10 🏛️Piazza Orazio Giustiniani 4 ⏰4–10pm Tue–Sun (only during exhibitions) 🌐museo macro.org

For much of the 20th century the Testaccio neighbourhood was a gutsy working-class quarter, dominated by its vast 19th-century slaughterhouse, the Mattatoio, which is considered to be one of the industrial architectural landmarks of the city. Testaccio has now become one of Rome's trendiest areas. The large halls of the Mattatoio have been transformed into a cutting-edge gallery hosting temporary modern and contemporary art exhibitions by established and emerging artists, and art-related events. Other parts of the complex are home to the Città dell'Altra Economia, which is committed to fair trade economies. It has an organic café and restaurant, a children's play area, a bookshop, crafts shops and alternative energy and recycling projects. There is also a fair trade market in Città dell'Altra Economia.

Santa Sabina

📍G8 🏛️Piazza Pietro d'Illiria 1 📞06-579 401 🚌23, 280, 716 Ⓜ️Circo Massimo ⏰8:15am–12:30pm & 3:30–6pm daily

High on the Aventine stands an early Christian basilica,

founded by Peter of Illyria in AD 425 and restored to its original simplicity in the early 20th century. Light filters through 9th-century windows upon a wide nave framed by white Corinthian columns supporting an arcade decorated with a marble frieze. Over the main door is a 5th-century blue and gold mosaic dedicatory inscription. The pulpit, carved choir and bishop's throne date from the 9th century.

The church was given to the Dominicans in the 13th century and in the nave is the magnificent mosaic tombstone of one of the first leaders of the order, Muñoz de Zamora (died 1300).

The side portico has 5th-century panelled doors carved from cypress wood, representing scenes from the Bible, including one of the earliest Crucifixions in existence.

Protestant Cemetery

📍 G10 🏛 Cimitero Acattolico, Via Caio Cestio 6 📞 06-574 1900 🚌 23, 280, 716 🚋 3 Ⓜ Piramide 🕐 9am-5pm Mon-Sat, 9am-1pm Sun (last adm: 30 mins before closing); donation expected

The peace of this well-tended cemetery, which is situated beneath the Aurelian Wall, is profoundly moving. As implied by its name, non-Catholics, mainly English and German, have been buried here since 1738. In the oldest part are the graves of the poet John Keats (died 1821), whose epitaph reads "Here lies One Whose Name was writ in Water", and his friend Joseph Severn (died 1879); not far away are the ashes of Percy Bysshe Shelley (died 1822). Goethe's son Julius is also buried here.

Pyramid of Caius Cestius

📍 H10 🏛 Piazzale Ostiense 🚌 23, 280, 716 🚋 3 Ⓜ Piramide 🕐 By appt 10:30am first Sat & Sun of the month (call 06-574 3193); all other Sat & Sun call 06-3996 7700

Caius Cestius, a wealthy *praetor* (senior Roman magistrate), died in 12 BC. His main claim to fame is his tomb, an imposing pyramid faced in white marble, set in the Aurelian Wall near Porta San Paolo. It stands 36 m (118 ft) high and, according to an inscription carved upon it, took 330 days to build. Unmistakable as a landmark, it must have looked almost as incongruous when it was built as it does today.

EAT & DRINK

Flavio Al Velavevodetto

This stellar trattoria, famed for its pasta dishes, backs onto Monte Testaccio; you can see the ancient amphorae through glass panels in the wall.

📍 G10 🏛 Via di Monte Testaccio 97 🌐 ristorante velavevodetto.it

Tram Depot

A friendly spot for an afternoon beer, and buzzing at *aperitivo* time in summer, this little café-bar (once part of a 1903 vintage tram) has quirky seating on the pavement.

📍 G9 🏛 Via Marmorata 13 📞 06-575 4406

TRASTEVERE

With its picturesque, higgledy-piggledy cobbled streets, mellow rose and ochre façades and intimate piazzas, bohemian Trastevere epitomizes a stranger's romantic notion of Rome. Shrines to the Madonna still protect tiny piazzas housing chic bars, restaurants and boutiques. In the evening this district becomes the centre of Rome's liveliest nightlife, with most of the action concentrated around Piazza Santa Maria in Trastevere. The area to the east of Viale di Trastevere is less gentrified, with warehouses dating back to the days when this was the home of the Tiber's dockers.

Cafés lining the banks of the Tiber River in Trastevere in summer ↓

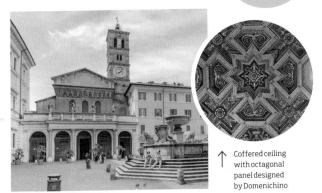

↑ Coffered ceiling with octagonal panel designed by Domenichino

↑ Santa Maria in Trastevere façade, with an octagonal fountain built in the late 17th century by Carlo Fontana in front

SANTA MARIA IN TRASTEVERE

📍F7 🏠 Piazza Santa Maria in Trastevere 📞 06-581 4802 🚌 H & 780 to Piazza San Sonnino, 23 & 280 along Lungotevere Sanzio 🚋 8 from Piazza Venezia 🕐 7:30am-9pm daily (8am-noon & 4-9pm Aug)

Probably the first official Christian place of worship to be built in Rome, this basilica became the focus of devotion to the Virgin Mary. Today it is famous for its splendid mosaics.

According to legend, the church was founded by Pope Callixtus I in the 3rd century, when Christianity was still a minority cult, on the site where a fountain of oil had miraculously sprung up on the day that Christ was born. Today's church is largely a 12th-century building, remarkable for its mosaics, in particular the apse mosaic of the Coronation of the Virgin and the six mosaics by Pietro Cavallini below it of the life of the Virgin, depicted with a touching realism. The 22 granite columns in the nave were taken from the ruins of ancient Roman buildings. Despite some 18th-century Baroque additions, Santa Maria has retained its medieval character.

EXPERIENCE MORE

Marta Ray

Come here for beautiful shoes, modern, eye-catching bags and purses, as well as accessories in colourful leather and suede. One of three locations in town.

📍F7 ⌂ Via del Moro 6 🌐 martaray.it

Pasticceria Valzani

This historic *pasticceria* and chocolate shop is ideal for sweet treats - the beautiful packages (and exquisite contents) make lovely gifts. Check out the mouthwatering displays at Easter and Christmas especially.

📍F7 ⌂ Via del Moro 37A 📞 06-580 3792

San Francesco a Ripa

📍F8 ⌂ Piazza San Francesco d'Assisi 88 📞 06-581 9020 🚌 H, 23, 44, 75, 280 🚋 8 ⏰ 7:30am-1pm & 2-7pm daily

St Francis of Assisi lived here in a hospice when he visited Rome in 1219, and his stone pillow and crucifix are preserved in his cell. The church was rebuilt by his follower, the nobleman Rodolfo Anguillara, who is portrayed on his tombstone wearing the Franciscan habit. Entirely rebuilt in the 1680s by Cardinal Pallavicini, the church is rich in sculptures. Particularly flamboyant are the 18th-century Rospigliosi and Pallavicini monuments in the transept chapel.

The Paluzzi-Albertoni Chapel (fourth on the left, along the nave) contains Bernini's breathtaking *Ecstasy of Beata Ludovica Albertoni*, completed in 1674.

Villa Sciarra

📍E8 ⌂ Via Calandrelli 35 🚌 44, 75 Park: ⏰ 9am-sunset daily

In Roman times the site of this small, attractive public park was a nymph's sanctuary. Shaded by trees, Villa Sciarra is a tranquil place to get away from the hustle and bustle of the surrounding streets. It is especially picturesque in spring when its wisterias are in full bloom. The paths through the park are decorated with Romantic follies, fountains and statues, and there are splendid views over the bastions of the Janiculum. It also contains the headquarters of the Italian Institute for Germanic Studies.

Ponte Sisto

📍F6 🚌 23, 280

Named after Pope Sixtus IV della Rovere (reigned 1471–84), who commissioned it, this bridge was built by Baccio Pontelli in 1475 to replace an ancient Roman bridge. The enterprising pope also commissioned the Sistine Chapel, the Hospital of Santo Spirito

→ Bernini's *Ecstasy of Beata Ludovica Albertoni* in San Francesco a Ripa

←

Ponte Sisto, with
the dome of St Peter's
in the background

and had many churches and monuments restored. This put him in great financial difficulties and he had to sell personal collections in order to finance his projects.

Casa della Fornarina

📍E6 🏛Via di Santa Dorotea 20 🚌23, 280

Not much is known about the life of Raphael's model and lover, La Fornarina, yet over the centuries she has acquired a name, Margherita Luti, and even a biography. Her father was a Sienese baker (*la fornarina* means "the baker's girl") and his shop was here in Trastevere near Raphael's frescoes in the Villa Farnesina.

Margherita earned a reputation as a "fallen woman" and Raphael, wishing to be absolved before dying, turned her away from his deathbed. After his death she took refuge in the convent of Santa Apollonia in Trastevere. She is assumed to have been the model for Raphael's portrait *La Donna Velata* housed in the Palazzo Pitti in Florence.

Santa Maria della Scala

📍E7 🏛Piazza della Scala 23 📞06-580 6233 🚌23, 280 🕐10am-1pm & 4-5:30pm daily

This church belongs to a time of great building activity that lasted about 30 years from the end of the 16th to the early 17th century. Its simple façade contrasts with a rich interior decorated with multicoloured marbles and a number of spirited Baroque altars and reliefs, as well as a few paintings, including Carlo Saraceni's Death of the Virgin. In 1849, the church was used as a hospital to treat the soldiers of Garibaldi's army.

JANICULUM

The highest of Rome's hills – though not one of the original seven – the Janiculum is a great place to go for a walk and views of the city, and can be approached from either the Vatican or Trastevere. The main focus is Piazzale Giuseppe Garibaldi, a wide, cobbled space with snack vans and a puppet show booth, at its busiest in the early evening as people gather to watch the sunset over the city. Head to Villa Farnesina for beautiful paintings and frescoes by Raphael and his pupils.

↓ Loggia of Cupid and Psyche

↑ Elegant, classical exterior of Villa Farnesina;
The Three Graces by Raphael *(inset)*

VILLA FARNESINA

📍E6 🏠 Via della Lungara 230 🚌 23, 280 to
Lungotevere 🕐 9am–2pm Mon–Sat & 9am–5pm
second Sun of every month 🚫 Aug 🌐 villafarnesina.it

A perfect example of Renaissance architecture, Villa Farnesina was built in
the early 16th century for the fabulously wealthy Sienese banker Agostino
Chigi, and served as a sophsticated retreat where he could entertain and
hold magnificent banquets.

Having established the headquarters
of his far-flung financial empire in Rome,
Agostino Chigi commissioned the villa
in 1508 from his compatriot, painter and
architect Baldassare Peruzzi. The simple,
harmonious design, with a central block
and projecting wings, made this one of
the earliest true Renaissance villas. The
decoration was carried out between 1510
and 1519 and has been restored. Peruzzi
frescoed some of the interiors himself.
Later, Sebastiano del Piombo, Raphael

and his pupils added more elaborate
works. The frescoes illustrate Classical
myths, and the vault of the main hall, the
Sala di Galatea, is adorned with astrological
scenes showing the position of the stars
at the time of Chigi's birth. Artists, poets,
cardinals, princes and the pope himself
were entertained here in magnificent style
by their wealthy and influential host. In 1577
the villa was bought by Cardinal Alessandro
Farnese. Since then, it has been known
as the Villa Farnesina.

EXPERIENCE MORE

Giuseppe and Anita Garibaldi Monuments

📍 D6 🏛 Piazzale Giuseppe Garibaldi
🚌 870

Dominating a huge open piazza on the summit of the Janiculum Hill is an equestrian statue of Giuseppe Garibaldi, hero of the Italian Unification. The statue and piazza commemorate the weeks in 1849 when Garibaldi and his men, based on the hill, fended off attacks from highly superior French forces, before finally being overwhelmed and escaping. In 2011, to mark the 150th anniversary of the Italian Republic, a low wall was erected, inscribed with the country's constitution.

A short distance away is a dramatic monument to Garibaldi's wife Anita, who fought alongside him. She is depicted on a leaping horse, a pistol in her right hand and her baby under her left arm.

Palazzo Corsini and Galleria Nazionale d'Arte Antica

📍 E6 🏛 Via della Lungara 10 🚌 23, 280
🕐 8:30am–7pm Mon, Wed–Sun 🌐 barberini corsini.org

The history of Palazzo Corsini is intimately entwined with that of Rome. Built for Cardinal Domenico Riario in 1510–12, it has boasted among its many distinguished guests Bramante, the young Michelangelo, Erasmus and Queen Christina of Sweden, who died here in 1689. The old palazzo was completely rebuilt for Cardinal Neri Corsini by Ferdinando Fuga in 1736. As Via della Lungara is too narrow for a good frontal view, Fuga designed

←
Dramatic equestrian statue of Anita Garibaldi riding into battle

the façade so it could be seen from an angle.

Palazzo Corsini houses the Galleria Nazionale d'Arte Antica, also known as Galleria Corsini. This outstanding collection includes paintings by Rubens, Van Dyck, Murillo, Caravaggio and Guido Reni, together with 17th- and 18th-century Italian regional art. The palazzo is also home to the Accademia dei Lincei, a learned society founded in 1603 that once included Galileo among its members.

In 1797 French General Duphot (the fiancé of Napoleon's sister Pauline) was killed here during a skirmish between papal troops and Republicans. The consequent French occupation of the city and the deportation of Pope Pius VI led to the proclamation of a short-lived Roman Republic (1798–9).

Botanical Gardens

📍 E6 🏛 Largo Cristina di Svezia 24, off Via Corsini
📞 06-4991 7108 🚌 23, 280 🕐 9am–6:30pm Mon–Sat (Nov–Mar: to 5:30pm)
🕐 Public hols

Sequoias, palm trees and collections of orchids and bromeliads are cultivated in Rome's Botanical Gardens (Orto Botanico). These tranquil gardens contain more than 7,000 plant species. Indigenous and exotic species are grouped to illustrate their botanical families and their adaptation to different climates and ecosystems. The gardens were originally part of the Palazzo Corsini but now belong to the University of Rome.

Porta Settimiana

♀ E6 ♙ Between Via della Scala and Via della Lungara 🚌 23, 280

This gate was built in 1498 by Pope Alexander VI Borgia to replace a minor passageway in the Aurelian Wall. The Porta Settimiana marks the start of Via della Lungara, a long road built in the early 16th century.

San Pietro in Montorio

♀ E7 ♙ Piazza San Pietro in Montorio 2
📞 06-581 3940 🚌 44, 75 🕐 **8am-noon & 3-4pm daily (times may vary in summer)**

San Pietro in Montorio – the church of St Peter on the Golden Hill – was founded in the Middle Ages near the spot where St Peter was presumed to have been crucified. It was rebuilt by order of Ferdinand and Isabella of Spain at the end of the 15th century, and decorated by outstanding artists of the Renaissance.

The single nave ends in a deep apse that once

contained Raphael's *Transfiguration*, now in the Vatican. Two wide chapels, one on either side of the nave, were decorated by some of Michelangelo's most famous pupils. The left-hand chapel was designed by Daniele da Volterra, who was also responsible for the altar painting, *The Baptism of Christ*. The chapel on the right was the work of Giorgio Vasari, who included a self-portrait (in black, on the left) in his altar painting, *The Conversion of St Paul*.

The first chapel to the right of the entrance contains a powerful *Flagellation*, by the Venetian artist Sebastiano del Piombo (1518); Michelangelo is said to have provided the original drawings. Work by Bernini and his followers can be seen in the second chapel on the left and in the flanking De Raymondi tombs.

Tempietto

♀ E7 ♙ Piazza San Pietro (in courtyard) 🚌 44, 75 🕐 **10am-6pm Tue-Sun**

Around 1502 Bramante completed what many consider to be the first true Renaissance building in Rome – the Tempietto, a perfectly circular Doric temple. The name means simply "little temple". Its circular shape echoes

EAT

Antico Arco

This chic restaurant has a short menu of gourmet Italian dishes made with top-notch ingredients, such as sea bass with Roman broccoli and black truffle. It is the ideal dining choice for a special occasion.

♀ D7 ♙ Piazzale Aurelio 7
 anticoarco.it

€€€

early Christian *martyria*, chapels built on the site of a saint's martyrdom. This was believed to be the place where St Peter was crucified.

Bramante chose the Doric order for the 16 columns surrounding the domed chapel. Above the columns is a Classical frieze and a delicate balustrade. Though the scale of the Tempietto is tiny, Bramante's masterly use of Classical proportions creates a satisfyingly harmonious whole. The Tempietto illustrates the great Renaissance dream that the city of Rome would once again relive its ancient glory.

VATICAN

With St Peter's basilica, the centre of the Roman Catholic faith, and the Vatican Museums, housing some of the world's greatest art collections, the Vatican is a must for pilgrims and art lovers. The area around the world's smallest sovereign state is full of busy streets lined with souvenir shops selling ecclesiastical memorabilia and hawkers flogging Sistine Chapel T-shirts and plaster Pietàs. Cobbled, pedestrianized Borgo Pio is the most attractive street, retaining some old-world charm and authentic places to eat.

St Peter's basilica seen across the Tiber River at sunset ↓

ST PETER'S

📍C4 🏛Piazza San Pietro 📞06-6988 3712 (Sacristy); 06-988 1662 (tourist info)
🚌23, 49, 70, 180, 492 Ⓜ️Ottaviano San Pietro 🕐Basilica: 7am-7pm daily Apr-Sep
(to 6:30pm mid-Oct-Mar); Treasury: 8am-7:30pm daily Apr-Sep (to 6:15pm Oct-Mar);
Grottoes: 8am-6pm daily Apr-Sep (to 5:30pm Oct-Mar); Dome: 8am-6pm daily Apr-
Sep (to 5pm Oct-Mar)

The centre of the Roman Catholic faith, St Peter's draws pilgrims from all
over the world. The magnificent basilica holds many precious works of art.

A shrine was erected in the 2nd century on the site where, according to Catholic tradition, St Peter was martyred and buried in AD 61. The first great basilica, ordered by Emperor Constantine, was constructed here in AD 349. By the 15th century it was falling down, so in 1506 Pope Julius II commissioned Bramante to replace the old church with a brand-new basilica. It took more than a hundred years to build and all the great architects and artists of the Roman Renaissance and Baroque had a hand in its design – not only Bramante, but Raphael, Bernini and Michelangelo. The basilica was finally completed in 1626 and is the world's second-largest church after Yamoussoukro in Côte d'Ivoire. Few are disappointed when they first enter the sumptuously decorated basilica beneath the vast dome designed by Michelangelo, the tallest dome in the world. For a fee you can go up into the dome. A broad ramp followed by a spiral staircase around the inside of the dome leads from the roof to the cupola, from where there are stunning views over the city and of Bernini's colonnade. Designed by Carlo Maderno, the travertine façade features Corinthian columns and a balustrade with 13 statues.

MASS AND AUDIENCE WITH THE POPE

The pope presides over Mass and addresses the crowds in St Peter's Square on Easter Day, Christmas Day and other major Christian festivals. General Audiences are usually held on Wednesdays (10-10.30am) in St Peter's Square (or in the Paul VI Audience Hall in bad weather). Get there very early if you want a chance of meeting or being blessed by the pope. Tickets to Papal Masses and General Audiences are free. To apply for a ticket visit www. vatican.va/various/prefettura/index_ en.html, and download the form. There is no email address and all applications must be faxed. See www.papalaudience. org/information for further details.

↑ Interior of St Peter's, showing the papal altar, with Bernini's magnificent baldacchino (sculpted canopy)

→
Michelangelo's breathtaking ceiling frescoes

VATICAN MUSEUMS

📍 C3 🏛 Città del Vaticano (entrance in Viale Vaticano) 🚌 49 to entrance, 23, 81, 492, 990 Ⓜ Ottaviano San Pietro, Cipro 🕐 9am–6pm Mon–Sat (last admission 4pm), 9am–2pm last Sun of month - free entry (last admission 12:30pm); low-cut or sleeveless clothing, shorts, mini-skirts and hats are not allowed 🚫 Religious and public hols 🌐 museivaticani.va

Home to the Sistine Chapel and Raphael Rooms as well as to one of the world's most important art collections, the Vatican Museums are housed in palaces originally built for Renaissance popes Julius II, Innocent VIII and Sixtus IV. Most of the later additions were made in the 18th century, when priceless works of art accumulated by earlier popes were first put on show. Strung along 7 km (over 4 miles) of corridors, these incredible collections form one of the world's largest museums.

Among the Vatican's greatest treasures are its superlative Greek and Roman antiquities, together with the magnificent artifacts excavated from Egyptian and Etruscan tombs during the 19th century. Some of Italy's leading artists, such as Raphael, Michelangelo and Leonardo da Vinci, are represented in the Pinacoteca (art gallery) and parts of the former palaces, where they were employed by popes to decorate sumptuous apartments and galleries. The absolute highlights of this complex of museums are the Sistine Chapel and the Raphael Rooms, which should not be missed.

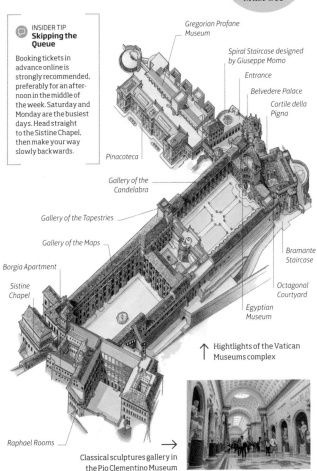

Gregorian Profane Museum

Spiral Staircase designed by Giuseppe Momo

Entrance

Belvedere Palace

Cortile della Pigna

Pinacoteca

Gallery of the Candelabra

Gallery of the Tapestries

Gallery of the Maps

Borgia Apartment

Sistine Chapel

Bramante Staircase

Octagonal Courtyard

Egyptian Museum

↑ Hightlights of the Vatican Museums complex

Raphael Rooms

→ Classical sculptures gallery in the Pio Clementino Museum

CASTEL SANT'ANGELO

📍E4 🏛Lungotevere Castello 50 🚌23, 40, 62 to Lungotevere Vaticano
or 34, 49, 87, 280, 492, 926, 990 to Piazza Cavour 🕐9am–7:30pm daily
(last adm: 6:30pm) 🌐castelsantangelo.beniculturali.it

A massive brick cylinder rising from the banks of the Tiber, Castel
Sant'Angelo began life in AD 139 as Emperor Hadrian's mausoleum.
Since then it has served as a medieval citadel, a prison and as the
residence of popes in times of political unrest.

The fortress takes its name from the
vision that Pope Gregory the Great had
of the Archangel Michael on this site. From
the dank cells in the lower levels to the
fine apartments of the Renaissance popes
above, Castel Sant-Angelo is now a 58-room
museum covering all aspects of the castle's
history. Highlights include the Sala Paolina,
decorated with illusionistic frescoes (1546–8)
by Pellegrino Tibaldi and Perin del Vaga, and
the armoury, which displays a wide range of
weaponry of the times. The castle's terrace,
scene of the last act of Puccini's opera Tosca,
offers great views in every direction.

PROTECTING THE POPE

The Vatican Corridor is
an elevated 800-m
(2,600-ft) passage that
leads from the Vatican
Palace to Castel Sant'
Angelo. It was built in
1277 to provide an
escape route when the
pope was in danger. The
pentagonal ramparts
built around the castle
during the 17th century
improved its defences in
times of siege.

←

Castel Sant'Angelo and the
bridge leading to it, adorned
with statues by Bernini

→

The richly adorned nave of the church of Santo Spirito in Sassia

EXPERIENCE MORE

Porta Santo Spirito

📍 D5 🏛 Via dei Penitenzieri 🚌 23, 34, 46, 62, 64, 98, 870, 881, 982

This gate is situated at what was once the southern limit of the "Leonine City", the area enclosed within walls by Pope Leo IV as a defence against the Saracens, who had sacked Rome in AD 845. The walls measure 3 km (2 miles) in circumference. Work on the walls started in AD 846. Pope Leo supervised the huge army of labourers personally, and the job was completed in four years. He then consecrated his massive feat of construction.

Since the time of Pope Leo the walls have needed much reinforcement and repair. The gateway visible today at Porta Santo Spirito was built by the architect Antonio da Sangallo the Younger in 1543–4. It is framed by two huge bastions that were added in 1564 by Pope Pius IV Medici. Sadly, Sangallo's design for a monu-mental entrance to the Vatican was never completed; the principal columns come to an end somewhat abruptly in a modern covering of cement.

Santo Spirito in Sassia

📍 D4 Via dei Penitenzieri 12 📞 06-687 9310 🚌 23, 34, 46, 62, 64, 98, 870, 881, 982 🕐 7:30am-noon & 3-6:30pm Mon-Sat, 9:30am-1pm & 3-6:30pm Sun

Built on the site of a church erected by King Ine of Wessex, who died in Rome in the 8th century, this church is the work of Antonio da Sangallo the Younger. It was rebuilt (1538–44) after the Sack of Rome left it in ruins in 1527. The façade was added under Pope Sixtus V (1585–90). The pretty bell tower is earlier, dating from the reign of Sixtus IV (1471–84).

Hospital of Santo Spirito

⊙ D5 **⌂** Borgo Santo Spirito 2 **🚌** 23, 34, 46, 62, 64 **⊙** Complex and chapel: for events only (call 06-6835 2433)

The oldest hospital in Rome, this is reputed to have been founded as a result of a nightmare experienced by Pope Innocent III (1198–1216). In the dream, an angel showed him the bodies of Rome's unwanted babies dredged up from the River Tiber in fishing nets. As a result, the pope hastened to build a hospice for sick paupers. In 1475 the hospital was reorganized by Pope Sixtus IV to care for the poor pilgrims expected for the Holy Year. Sixtus's hospital was a radical building. Cloisters divided the different types of patients; one area is still reserved for orphans and their nurses.

In order to guarantee anonymity, unwanted infants were passed through a revolving barrel-like contraption called the *rota*, still visible to the left of the central entrance in Borgo Santo Spirito. Martin Luther, who visited in 1511, was shocked by the number of abandoned children he saw, believing them to be "the sons of the pope himself".

In the centre, under the hospital's conspicuous drum, is an octagonal chapel, where Mass was said for patients. This room can be visited by prior arrangment, while the rest of the building still functions as a hospital.

The Borgo

⊙ D4 **🚌** 23, 34, 40, 62

The Borgo's name derives from the German *burg*, meaning "town". Rome's Borgo is where the first pilgrims to St Peter's were housed in hostels and hospices, often for quite lengthy periods. The first of these foreign colonies, called "schools", was founded in AD 725 by a Saxon, King Ine of Wessex, who wished to live a life of penance and to be buried near the Tomb of St Peter. These days hotels and hostels have made the Borgo a colony of international pilgrims once again. Much of the area's character was lost after redevelopment in the 1930s, but it is still enjoyable to stroll the old narrow streets on either side of Via della Conciliazione.

Did You Know?

Raphael and Michelangelo count among the Borgo area's most famous past residents.

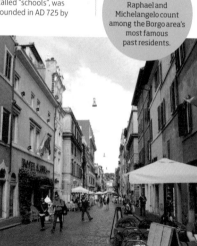

Palazzo del Commendatore

D4 **Borgo Santo Spirito 3** **06-6835 2353** **23, 34, 46, 62, 64** **Courtyard open to public**

As director of the Hospital of Santo Spirito, the Commendatore not only oversaw the running of the hospital, he was also responsible for its estates and revenues. This important post was originally given to members of the pope's family.

The palazzo, built next door to the hospital, has a spacious 16th-century frescoed loggia appropriate to the dignity and sobriety of its owners. The frescoes represent the story of the founding of the Hospital of Santo Spirito. To the left of the entrance is the Spezieria, or Pharmacy. This still has the wheel used for grinding the bark of the cinchona tree to produce the drug quinine, first introduced here in 1632 by Jesuits from Peru as a cure for malaria.

Above the courtyard is a splendid clock (1827). The dial is divided into six; it was not until 1846 that the familiar division of the day

Street lined with shops and restaurants in the historic Borgo area near the Vatican

into two periods of 12 hours was introduced in Rome by Pope Pius IX.

Santa Maria in Traspontina

D4 **Via della Conciliazione 14** **06-6880 6451** **23, 34, 62, 64** **6:30am–noon & 4-7:15pm Mon-Sat, 7:30am-1pm Sun**

The church occupies the site of an ancient Roman pyramid, believed in the Middle Ages to have been the Tomb of Romulus. The pyramid was destroyed by Pope Alexander VI Borgia, but representations of it survive in the bronze doors at the entrance to St Peter's and in a Giotto triptych housed in the Vatican Pinacoteca.

The present church was begun in 1566 to replace an earlier one which had been in the line of fire of the cannons defending Castel Sant'Angelo during the Sack of Rome in 1527. The papal artillery officers therefore insisted that the dome of the new church should be as low as possible, so it was built without a supporting drum. The first chapel to the right is dedicated to the gunners' patron saint, Santa Barbara, and is decorated with war-like motifs. In the third chapel on the left are two columns, popularly

thought to be the ones which SS Peter and Paul were bound to before going to their martyrdom nearby.

EAT & DRINK

Despite its reputation as something of a culinary wasteland, the Vatican area has a number of good places to enjoy a well-earned plate of food and a restorative glass of wine after visiting the museums.

Dal Toscano

C3 **Via Germanico 58** **ristorantedaltoscano.it**

Franchi

D3 **Via Cola di Rienzo 200** **06-686 5564**

Il Simposio

E3 **Piazza Cavour 16** **ilsimposioroma.it**

VIA VENETO

The focus of the decadent and glamorous night scene of the late 1950s and 60s that inspired Fellini's film *La Dolce Vita*, Via Veneto is but a shadow of its former self, though the street retains its elegance and is home to some of the city's most luxurious hotels. The fascinating, though macabre, Capuchin Crypt, with thousands of human bones as well as mummified corpses decorating its walls and ceilings, comes as a surprise underneath the 17th-century Santa Maria della Concezione church.

The curving Via Veneto, lined with cafés, restaurants and hotels

EXPERIENCE

Via Veneto

📍 J3 🚌 52, 53, 63, 80, 116, 119, 160 to Piazza Barberini Ⓜ Barberini

Via Veneto descends in a lazy curve from the Porta Pinciana to Piazza Barberini, lined in its upper reaches with exuberant late 19th-century hotels and canopied pavement cafés. It was laid out in 1879 over a large estate sold by the Ludovisi family in the great building boom of Rome's first years as capital of Italy. Palazzo Margherita, intended to be the new Ludovisi family palazzo, was completed in 1890. It now houses the American embassy. In the 1960s this was the most glamorous street in Rome, its cafés patronized by film stars and plagued by paparazzi. Most of the people drinking in the cafés today are tourists, as film stars now seem to prefer the bohemian atmosphere of Trastevere or the luxury of the Parioli neighbourhood.

Santa Maria della Vittoria

📍 K3 🏠 Via XX Settembre 17 📞 06-4274 0571 🚌 60, 61, 62, 492, 910 Ⓜ Repubblica 🕐 8:30am-noon & 3:30-6pm daily

This intimate Baroque church has a lavishly decorated candlelit interior. It contains one of Bernini's most ambitious sculptural works, *Ecstasy of St Teresa* (1646), the centrepiece of the Cornaro Chapel, built to resemble a miniature theatre. It even has an audience: sculptures of the chapel's benefactor, Cardinal Federico Cornaro, and his ancestors sit in boxes, as if watching the scene in front of them. Visitors may be shocked or thrilled by the apparently physical nature of St Teresa's ecstasy. She lies on a cloud, her mouth half open and her eyelids closed, with rippling drapery covering her body. Looking over her with a smile, which from different angles can appear either tender or cruel, is a curly-haired angel holding an arrow with which he is about to pierce the saint's body for a second time. The marble figures are framed and illuminated by rays of divine light materialized in bronze.

Palazzo Barberini

📍 J4 🏠 Via delle Quattro Fontane 13 🚌 52, 53, 61, 62, 63, 80, 116, 492, 590 Ⓜ Barberini 🕐 8:30am-7pm Tue-Sun 🔒 1 Jan, 25 Dec 🌐 barberinicorsini.org

When Maffeo Barberini became Pope Urban VIII in 1623 he planned a grand palace for his family on the fringes of the city. Architect Carlo Maderno designed it as a rural villa, with wings into the surrounding gardens. Maderno died in 1629 and Bernini took over, assisted by Borromini. The pediments on some of the top-floor windows, and the oval staircase inside, are almost certainly by Borromini. The most striking of the sumptuous rooms is the Gran Salone, with an illusionistic ceiling fresco by Pietro da Cortona. The palazzo also houses paintings from the 13th to the 16th centuries, with notable works by Filippo Lippi, Caravaggio and El Greco as well as Guido Reni's *Beatrice Cenci*, the young woman executed for planning her father's murder, and *La Fornarina*, traditionally thought to be a portrait of Raphael's mistress, although not necessarily painted by him.

Fontana del Tritone

📍 J4 🏠 Piazza Barberini 🚌 52, 53, 61, 62, 63, 80, 116, 119 Ⓜ Barberini

In the centre of busy Piazza Barberini is one of Bernini's liveliest creations, the Triton Fountain. It was created for Pope Urban VIII Barberini in 1642, shortly after the completion of his palace on the ridge above. Acrobatic dolphins stand on their heads, twisting their tails together to support a huge scallop shell on which the sea god Triton kneels, blowing a spindly column of water up into the air through a conch shell.

BEFORE YOU GO

Forward planning is essential to any successful trip. Be prepared for all eventualities by considering the following points before you travel.

AT A GLANCE

CURRENCY
Euro (EUR)

AVERAGE DAILY SPEND

SAVE
€50

SPEND
€100

SPLURGE
€200+

Bottled Water
€1.30

Coffee
€1.50

Beer
€5

Dinner for Two
€60

ESSENTIAL PHRASES

Hello	Buongiorno/Ciao
Goodbye	Arrivederci
Please	Per favore
Thank you	Grazie
Do you speak English?	Parla inglese?
I don't understand	Non ho capito

ELECTRICITY SUPPLY

Power sockets are type F and L, fitting two- and three-pronged plugs. Standard voltage is 220-230v.

Passports and Visas

EU nationals and citizens of the UK, US, Canada, Australia and New Zealand do not need visas for stays of up to three months. Consult your nearest Italian embassy or check the **Polizia di Stato** website if you are travelling from outside these areas.
Polizia di Stato
W poliziadistato.it

Travel Safety Advice

Visitors can get up-to-date travel safety information from the **UK Foreign and Commonwealth Office**, the **US State Department** and the **Australian Department of Foreign Affairs and Trade**.
AUS
W smartraveller.gov.au
UK
W gov.uk/foreign-travel-advice
US
W travel.state.gov

Customs Information

An individual is permitted to carry the following within the EU for personal use:
Tobacco products: 800 cigarettes, 400 cigarillos, 200 cigars or 1 kg of smoking tobacco.
Alcohol: 10 litres of alcoholic beverages above 22% strength, 20 litres of alcoholic beverages below 22% strength, 90 litres of wine (60 litres of which can be sparkling wine) and 110 litres of beer.
Cash: if you plan to enter or leave the EU with €10,000 or more in cash (or the equivalent in other currencies) you must declare it to the customs authorities.
Outside the EU limits vary, so check restrictions before departing.

Insurance

It is wise to take out an insurance policy covering theft, loss of belongings, medical problems, cancellation and delays. EU citizens are eligible for free emergency medical care in Italy provided they have a valid **EHIC** (European Health Insurance Card). Visitors from outside the EU must arrange their own private medical insurance.
EHIC
ⓦ gov.uk/european-health-insurance-card

Vaccinations

No inoculations are needed for Italy.

Booking Accommodation

Rome offers a huge variety of accommodation, comprising luxury five-star hotels, family-run B&Bs, budget hostels and private apartment rentals. A list of accommodation to suit all needs can be found on the ENIT (Italy's national tourist board) website.

During peak season lodgings fill up and prices become inflated, so book in advance.

All accommodation adds the city tourist tax to its rates. This varies between €3 and €7 per night (depending on the hotel category) for a maximum of ten nights. Always check if the city tax is included in the rate quoted to you.

Under Italian law, hotels are required to register guests at police headquarters and issue a receipt of payment (ricevuta fiscale), which you must keep until you leave Italy.

Money

Most establishments accept major credit, debit and prepaid currency cards. Contactless payments are becoming increasingly common in Rome, but it's always a good idea to carry some cash for smaller items such as coffee, gelato, pizza-by-the-slice, and when visiting markets or more remote areas.

Travellers with Specific Needs

Rome's historic towns and cobbled streets are ill-equipped for disabled access. Many buildings do not have wheelchair access or lifts. Always call ahead to ensure that your needs will be met.
CO.IN. Sociale provides information and general assistance for travellers with mobility issues.

Assistance at airports can be arranged by notifying your airline company or travel agent of your particular needs in advance of your trip. **ADR Assistance** can coordinate assistance at Rome's Ciampino or Fiumicino or airports. Train travellers with Trenitalia can arrange special reservations and assistance at stations.
ADR Assistance
ⓦ adr.it
CO.IN.Sociale
ⓦ coinsociale.it

Language

The level of English spoken in Rome varies. Many of those working in the city's major tourist areas speak good English. However, a little knowledge of the local language goes a long way, and locals appreciate visitors' efforts to speak Italian, even if only a few words.

Closures

Lunchtime Most shops, churches and some small businesses shut for a few hours in the afternoon.

Monday Many museums and restaurants close all day.

Sunday Restaurants usually close for lunch. Churches and cathedrals forbid tourists from visiting during Mass, and public transport runs a reduced service.

Public holidays Shops, churches and museums either close early or for the day.

GETTING AROUND

Whether exploring Rome's historic centre by foot or making use of the city's public transport, here is all you need to know to navigate the city.

AT A GLANCE

PUBLIC TRANSPORT COSTS
Tickets are valid on all forms of public transport in Rome.

ONE-WAY

€1.50

100 mins transfers included

DAY TICKET

€7

Unlimited travel

3-DAY TICKET

€18

Unlimited travel

SPEED LIMIT

MOTORWAY	DUAL CARRIAGEWAYS
130 km/h (80 mph)	**110** km/h (70 mph)

SECONDARY ROAD	URBAN AREAS
90 km/h (50 mph)	**50** km/h (30 mph)

Arriving by Air

Rome has two airports, Fiumicino and Ciampino, both served by international flights and with excellent transport links to the city centre.

Train Travel

International Train Travel

Regular high-speed international trains connect Italy to the main towns and cities in Austria, Germany, France and Eastern Europe. Reservations for these services are essential and tickets are booked up quickly. You can buy tickets and passes for multiple international journeys via **Eurail** or **Interrail**; however, you may still need to pay an additional reservation fee depending on which rail service you travel with. Always check that your pass is valid before boarding.
Eurail W eurail.com
Interrail W interrail.eu

Regional and Local Trains

Trenitalia is the main operator in Italy. Tickets can be bought online but there are only a fixed number available so book ahead. For travelling between cities, **Italo Treno** (NTV) and **Trenitalia** (FS) also offer a high-speed rail service. Reservations are essential. Rome's main stations are Termini and Tiburtina. There is a useful city line to Ostia Antica and Ostia Lido from Stazione Porta San Paolo, next to the Piramide Metro station.

Tickets must be validated by stamping them before boarding. Machines are positioned at the entrance to platforms in railway stations for this purpose. Heavy fines are levied if you are caught with an unvalidated ticket.
Italo Treno W italotreno.it
Trenitalia W trenitalia.com

Public Transport

ATAC is Rome's main public transport authority. Timetables, ticket information, transport maps, and more can be obtained from ATAC kiosks, the customer service office or the ATAC website.

ATAC

w atac.roma.it

Tickets

Tickets (biglietti) are available from kiosks, stations, bars, newsstands, or any shop with the ATAC sticker in the window. Tickets cannot be bought on board – they must be bought in advance (there are automatic ticket machines at main bus stops and Metro stations that take coins) and must be validated on the day of travel.

Tickets are valid on all modes of public transport, including buses, trams, Metro, and local train lines. Regular one-way tickets (BIT) valid for 75 minutes cost €1.50, day tickets (BIG) cost €7, three-day tickets (BTI) cost €18 and weekly passes (CIS) are €24. Children under 10 travel for free with an adult.

Metro

Rome's Metro (Metropolitana) has three lines – A, B and C. Line A runs from west to southeast and Line B runs from northeast to south. A and B meet at Termini station, and A and C at San Giovanni. Regional rail services connect with the Metro to serve the surrounding areas and the airports. Line C runs from Pantano station to San Giovanni, where it links with Line A. Trains run every 4–10 minutes 5:30am–11:30pm daily, and 5:30am–1:30am on Friday and Saturday nights.

On street level, Metro stations are clearly marked by red and white "M" signs. Use the Metro maps in stations to identify which line you need and the terminus you will be heading for, then follow the signs in the station. At the station, insert your ticket through the barrier to access the platform. Keep your ticket for inspection. Screens on the platform show the waiting time for the next train. Look out for your stop, as it may not be announced.

Trams

Trams cover the outskirts of the city centre and are a good way to get to the main sights while avoiding the crowded centre. The most useful are No. 2 (to MAXXI) and No. 19 (connecting Vatican City with Villa Borghese). Tram stops display the tram numbers that serve them and a list of stops on each route. Approaching trams display the route number and their destination.

Useful routes include Route 2 (along Via Flaminio) and Route 8 (between Largo Argentina and Trastevere). Trams operate 5:30am–10:30pm or midnight daily, depending on the route (Route 8 runs until 3am on Friday and Saturday nights). Tickets must be stamped on board in the yellow machines.

Buses

Buses cover most of the city. When not stuck in traffic they are a quick way to reach the main sights and attractions of Rome. The main bus terminus is on Piazza dei Cinquecento outside Termini station, but there are other major route hubs throughout the city, most usefully those at Piazza del Risorgimento and Piazza Venezia. Bus stops display the bus numbers that serve them and a list of stops on each route. Regular services generally run every 10 to 20 minutes. After 11:30pm a night bus service operates until 5.15am. Night buses are marked with the letter "N" (for notturno) before the route number. Buses must be flagged down. Enter at the front or back doors and exit via the middle door (although people may not always adhere to this system).

Tickets must be stamped in the yellow machines located at the front or back of the bus. Press the button to request a stop. For day trips, COTRAL blue buses run from several Rome terminals out into the suburbs and surrounding countryside.

Long-Distance Bus Travel

Long-distance coaches terminate at Tiburtina, which is the city's main coach station. Tickets and information for coaches to European cities are available from the **Eurolines**, **Flixbus** or **Italybus** websites.

Local buses, serving villages and towns within the Lazio region, are run by **COTRAL**. All bus stations used by COTRAL in Rome are linked to Metro stations. Tickets are purchased on the spot and cannot be booked in advance.

Eurolines W eurolines.com
Flixbus W flixbus.it
Italybus W italybus.it

Guided Bus Tours

City Sightseeing Roma offers hop-on-hop-off tours of the city aboard double-decker buses with audio guides in eight languages. Tours run daily with a first departure at 9am and a last departure at 7pm. The full tour lasts 1 hour 40 minutes, and buses run with a frequency of 15 to 20 minutes. Buses can be boarded at any of the eight stops, which include the Colosseum, Trevi Fountain, Piazza Barberini and the Vatican. You can also buy "combo" tickets that include the Colosseum and the Vatican, or night tours. The **Roma Cristiana** bus is a tour with a Christian emphasis. It runs from Termini to Piazza San Pietro with stops close to religious sights, and includes audio guides.

City Sightseeing Roma
W roma.city-sightseeing. it
Roma Cristiana
W operaromanapellegrinaggi.org

Taxis

Taxis in Rome are some of the most expensive in Europe and not all accept credit cards. They cannot be hailed; take one at an official taxi stand at stations, main piazzas or close to key tourist sights – the most useful are at Termini, Piazza Venezia, Piazza di Spagna, Piazza del Popolo and Piazza Barberini. You can also reserve online or by phone. When you order a taxi by phone, the meter will run from your call. Official taxis are white, have a "taxi" sign on the roof and their official taxi license number on the doors. Alternatively, well-known taxi apps such as UBER also operate in Rome. Extra charges are added for each piece of luggage placed in the boot, for rides between 10pm and 7am, on Sundays and public holidays, and for journeys to and from airports. Report any problems with taxi drivers by calling 060608.

Chiama Taxi 060609
Radiotaxi 3570 W 3570.it

Driving

Driving in Rome is not recommended – roads are congested and parking is extremely difficult, even for locals.

Driving to Rome

Rome is easily reachable from other European countries via E-roads, the International European Road Network connecting major roads across national borders within Europe, or by national (N) and secondary (SS) roads from neighbouring France, Switzerland, Austria and Slovenia.

Tolls are payable on most motorways (autostrade), and payment is made at the end of the journey in cash, by credit card or pre-paid magnetic VIA cards, available from tobacconists and the **ACI** (Automobile Club d'Italia). If you wish to avoid toll roads, there is almost always an alternative route signposted. If you bring your own foreign-registered car to Italy, you must carry a Green Card, the vehicle's registration documents and a valid driver's licence.

ACI W aci.it

Car Rental

To rent a car in Italy you must be over 21 and have held a valid driver's licence with no points for at least one year. Driving licences issued by any of the European Union member states are valid throughout the EU, including Italy. If visiting from outside the EU, you may need to apply for an International Driving Permit (IDP). Check with your local automobile association before you travel.

Driving in Rome

City centre streets are designated ZTL (*Zona a Traffico Limitato*) which means that only residents can drive and park there. Those arriving by car are advised to leave it in a car park outside the city centre. The **European Car Parking Guide** and **Saba** list free car parks on Rome's periphery. There are also car parks located near Villa Borghese and Piazza Partigiani. Look for a white "P" sign on a blue background. Metered parking is permitted in parking spaces identified by a white line from 8am until 8pm. If your vehicle is towed, call the municipal police. You can reach them by dialling 06-0606. Tell them where you parked and they will direct you to the nearest tow lot. Once you have located your vehicle, you will have to pay a fee to retrieve it as well as pay for the parking violation.

European Car Parking Guide
Ⓦ car-parking.eu/italy/rome/pr
Saba Ⓦ sabait.it

Rules of the Road

Drive on the right, use the left lane only for passing, and yield to traffic from the right. Seat belts are required for all passengers in the front and back, and heavy fines are levied for using a mobile phone while driving. During the day dipped headlights are compulsory when driving on motorways, dual carriageways and on all out-of-town roads. A red warning triangle and fluorescent vests must be carried at all times, for use in the event of an emergency.

If you have an accident or breakdown, switch on your hazard warning lights and place a warning triangle 50 m (55 yd) behind your vehicle. In the event of a breakdown, call the ACI emergency number (803 116) or the emergency services (112 or 113). The ACI will tow any foreign-registered car to the nearest ACI-affiliated garage for free.

The legal drink-drive limit is strictly enforced. If you are drinking alcohol, use public transport or take a taxi.

Hitchhiking

Hitchhiking (*autostop*) is illegal on motorways, and is not commonplace in large cities such as Rome. In more rural areas it is a common transport method for travellers on a budget. Always consider your own safety before entering an unknown vehicle.

Cycle and Scooter Hire

Cycling in Rome can be a challenging task due to the city's hilly nature, the heavy traffic and the lack of bike paths. If you are not up for urban cycling, a ride in Villa Borghese park can be a healthier and more enjoyable alternative. Bikes, tandems and rickshaws can all be hired by the entrance of the Pincio Gardens. You can rent bicycles, motorcycles and scooters hourly or by the day. You may have to leave your passport with the rental shop as a deposit, and you must have a valid licence to hire a scooter or motorcycle. **Bici & Baci** and **Barberini Scooters for Rent** offer bike and scooter rental by the hour and by the day.

Motorcyclists, scooter drivers and their passengers must wear helmets by law; these can be rented from most hire shops. Unless you are an experienced moped or scooter rider, it is wiser not to ride in Rome.

Barberini Scooters for Rent
Ⓦ rentscooter.it
Bici & Baci Ⓦ bicibaci.com

Walking

Wandering through Rome's historic centre is one of the most enjoyable aspects of the city. Much of the city is made up of narrow lanes and alleys, which are impenetrable to buses. You can take in the architectural details, absorb the streetlife and peek into any church, shop or bar that catches your interest. You can easily visit several of the main tourist sights in a few hours.

PRACTICAL INFORMATION

A little local know-how goes a long way in Rome. Here you can find all the essential advice and information you will need during your stay.

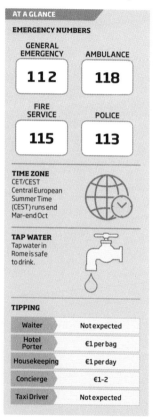

AT A GLANCE

EMERGENCY NUMBERS

GENERAL EMERGENCY	AMBULANCE
112	**118**

FIRE SERVICE	POLICE
115	**113**

TIME ZONE
CET/CEST
Central European Summer Time (CEST) runs end Mar–end Oct

TAP WATER
Tap water in Rome is safe to drink.

TIPPING

Waiter	Not expected
Hotel Porter	€1 per bag
Housekeeping	€1 per day
Concierge	€1–2
Taxi Driver	Not expected

Personal Security

Bag-snatching scooter drivers are a problem, so hold bags on the inside of the pavement where possible, especially in crowded tourist areas. Pickpockets are common on public transport, so be careful on popular bus routes such as 23, 40 and 64. Keep your belongings in a safe place and with you at all times. If you have anything stolen, report the crime within 24 hours to the nearest police station and take ID with you. Get a copy of the crime report (denuncia) to make an insurance claim. Contact your embassy if you have your passport stolen, or in the event of a serious crime or accident.

Health

Seek medicinal supplies and advice for minor ailments from pharmacies (farmacia). You can find details of the nearest 24-hour service on all pharmacy doors. Emergency medical care in Italy is free for all EU and Australian citizens. If you have an EHIC card, be sure to present this as soon as possible. You may have to pay after treatment and reclaim the money later. For visitors coming from outside the EU and Australia, payment of hospital and other medical expenses is the patient's responsibility. It is therefore important to arrange comprehensive medical insurance before travelling.

Smoking, Alcohol and Drugs

Smoking is banned in enclosed public places. Possession of narcotics is prohibited and could result in a prison sentence. Italians tend to drink only with meals and are unlikely to be seen drunk – obvious drunkenness is frowned upon. Italy has a strict limit of 0.05 per cent BAC (blood alcohol content) for drivers. This means that you cannot drink more than a small beer or a small glass of wine if you plan to drive. For drivers with less than three years' driving experience the limit is 0.

ID

By law you must carry identification with you at all times in Italy. A photocopy of your passport photo page (and visa if applicable) should suffice. If you are stopped by the police you may be asked to present the original document within 12 hours.

Local Customs

You can be fined for dropping litter, sitting on monument steps or eating or drinking outside churches, historic monuments and public buildings. It is an offence to swim or bathe in public fountains. Illegal street traders operate in many of Rome's main tourist areas; avoid buying from them as you could be fined by the local police.

Visiting Churches and Cathedrals

Entrance to churches is free, but you may be charged a small fee to see a certain area, such as a chapel, cloister or underground ruins. Strict dress codes apply: cover your torso and upper arms, and ensure shorts and skirts cover your knees. Shoes must be worn.

Mobile Phones and Wi-Fi

Wi-Fi is generally widely available, and cafés, bars, restaurants and some cultural venues will usually allow you to use their Wi-Fi on the condition that you make a purchase. Visitors travelling to Italy with EU tariffs will be able to use their devices abroad without being affected by roaming charges. Users will be charged the same rates for data, voice calls and SMS services as they would pay at home.

Post

Stamps are sold in kiosks and tobacconists. The Vatican City and San Marino have their own post systems and stamps. Only letters bearing San Marino or Vatican stamps can be posted in San Marino and Vatican postboxes. Italian post is notorious for its unreliability. Letters and postcards can take anything between four days and two weeks to arrive.

Taxes and Refunds

VAT (IVA) is usually 22 per cent. Under certain conditions, non-EU citizens can claim a rebate. Either claim the rebate before you buy (show your passport to the shop assistant and complete a form), or claim it retrospectively by presenting a customs officer with your receipts as you leave. Stamped receipts will be sent back to the vendor to issue a refund.

Discount Cards

There are a number of visitor passes and discount cards available for Rome. It is worth considering carefully how many of the offers are likely to take advantage of before purchasing one of these.

The two-day or three-day **Roma Pass** (€28/€38.50) includes public transport, entry to two museums or archaeological sites and discounts for various exhibitions and events. The **Omnia Rome and Vatican Pass** (€113 for three days) offers a similar package, but also includes the Vatican Museums. Many national and city museums offer free entry to under 18s, and discounts for students. During the *Beni Culturali* (Ministry for Culture and Heritage week) in April, admission to all state-run sites is free.

Roma Pass
W romapass.it
Omnia Rome and Vatican Pass
W romeandvaticanpass.com

INDEX

ACKNOWLEDGMENTS

Dorling Kindersley would like to extend special thanks to the following people for their contribution: Anamika Bhandari, Syed Mohammad Farhan, Shanker Prasad, Rohit Rojal.

The publisher would like to thank the following for their kind permission to reproduce their photographs:

Key: a-above; b-below/bottom; c-centre; f-far; l-left; r-right; t-top

123RF.com: gonewiththewind 8br.

Alamy Stock Photo: Vito Arcomano 56tl, 78tr, 89t; Azoor Photo 89cr; Gabriele Dessì 58b; Adam Eastland 28bl, 88b, 95br; freeartist 4-5b; imageBROKER 87tl; Boris Karpinski 69br; John Kellerman 70tl; Kosobu 76tl; Martin Thomas Photography 71br; Hercules Milas 7tl, 37b; Nikreates 21t; Danilo Poccia 50bl; RealyEasyStar / Daniele Bellucci 54b; John Rees 17bl;

Robertharding / Neale Clark 93crb; Rudi1976 13tl; Jozef Sedmak 97t; Eckhard Supp 48t; Glyn Thomas 66b; Universal Images Group North America LLC / DeAgostini 86br; Stefano Valeri 74b; Ivan Vdovin 60tc; Sebastian Wasek 33br.

AWL Images: Marco Bottigelli 12b; Francesco Iacobelli 2t; Maurizio Rellini 3tl, 20b, 27tl.

Bridgeman Images: De Agostini Picture Library / G. Dagli Orti / Painted terracotta Sarcophagus of the Spouses, from Cerveteri, Rome province, Italy, detail, 520 B.C. 38cra.

Dorling Kindersley: Demetrio Carrasco 36crb; John Heseltine 47tr, 100b.

Dreamstime.com: Leonid Andronov 44b; Christophefaugere 41tl; Jacqueline Cooper 36t; Danflcreativo 80b; Rostislav Glinsky 19t; Anna Hristova 98br; Ixuskmitl 85tl; Dragan

Jovanovic 18bl; Luxerendering 75tl, 75tc; Marcovarro 46br, 85tr; Marinv 72tr; Marsana 57bl; Antony Mcaulay 67tr; Roland Nagy 55crb; William Perry 42b; Photogolfer 94t; Marek Poplawski 45tr, 61bl; Gianluca Rasile 24br; Rinofelino 68b; Valerio Rosati 38bl, 45tl; Jozef Sedmak 11tr, 62b, 64tl; Tupungato 29tl; Stefano Valeri 16t.

Getty Images: Domingo Leiva 6b; joe daniel price 96bl; REDA&CO 34b, 84b.ç

iStockphoto.com: bwzenith 82tl; Francesco Cantone 52tl; fotoVoyager 92b; Yves Grau 70tr; PaoloGaetano 90bl; Romaoslo 17cr; Violetastock 35t; zorazhuang 14clb.

Robert Harding Picture Library: Terrance Klassen 26b.

Photo Scala, Florence: Andrea Jemolo 30tr.

For further information see: www.dkimages.com

PHRASE BOOK

IN EMERGENCY

Help!	**Aiuto!**	eye-**yoo**-toh
Stop!	**Ferma!**	fair-**mah**
Call a doctor	**Chiama un medico**	kee-**ah**-mah oon **meh**-dee-koh
Call an ambulance	**Chiama un' ambulanza**	kee-**ah**-mah oon am-boo-**lan**-tsa
Call the police	**Chiama la polizia**	kee-**ah**-mah lah pol-ee-**tsee**-ah
Call the fire brigade	**Chiama i pompieri**	kee-**ah**-mah ee pom-pee-**air**-ee
Where is the telephone?	**Dov'è il telefono?**	dov-**eh**eel teh-**leh**-foh-noh?
The nearest hospital?	**L'ospedale più vicino?**	loss-peh-**dah**-leh pee-**chee**-**oo**vee--noh?

COMMUNICATION ESSENTIALS

Yes/No	**Si/No**	**see**/noh
Please	**Per favore**	pair fah-**vor**-eh
Thank you	**Grazie**	**grah**-tsee-eh
Excuse me	**Mi scusi**	mee **skoo**-zee
Hello	**Buon giorno**	bwon **jor**-noh
Goodbye	**Arrivederci**	ah-ree-veh-**dair**-chee
yesterday	**ieri**	ee-**air**-ee
today	**oggi**	**oh**-jee
tomorrow	**domani**	doh-**mah**-nee
here	**qui**	**kwee**
there	**la**	**lah**
What?	**Quale?**	**kwah**-leh?
When?	**Quando?**	**kwan**-doh?
Why?	**Perchè?**	pair-**keh**?
Where?	**Dove?**	**doh**-veh?

USEFUL PHRASES

| How are you? | **Come sta?** | **koh**-meh stah? |
| Very well, thank you. | **Molto bene, grazie.** | **moll**-toh **beh**-neh **grah**-tsee-eh |

Pleased to meet you.	**Piacere di conoscerla.**	pee-ah-**chair**-eh dee coh-**noh**-shair-lah
See you soon.	**A più tardi.**	ah pee-oo **tar**-dee
That's fine.	**Va bene.**	va **beh**-neh
Where is/are ...?	**Dov'è/Dove sono...?**	dov-**eh**/doveh **soh**noh?
How long does it take to get to ...?	**Quanto tempo ci vuole per andare a ...?**	**kwan**-toh **tem**-poh chee voo-oh-leh pair an-**dar**-eh ah...?
How do I get to ...?	**Come faccio per arrivare a ...?**	**koh**-meh **fah**-choh pair arri-**var**-eh ah...?
Do you speak English?	**Parla inglese?**	**par**-lah een-**gleh**-zeh?
I don't understand.	**Non capisco.**	non ka-**pee**-skoh
Could you speak more slowly, please?	**Può parlare più lentamente, per favore?**	pwoh par-**lah**-reh pee-**oo**len-ta-**men**-teh fah-**vor**-eh?
I'm sorry.	**Mi dispiace.**	mee dee-spee-**ah**-cheh

USEFUL WORDS

big	**grande**	**gran**-deh
small	**piccolo**	**pee**-koh-loh
hot	**caldo**	**kal**-doh
cold	**freddo**	**fred**-doh
good	**buono**	**bwoh**-noh
bad	**cattivo**	kat-**tee**-voh
open	**aperto**	ah-**pair**-toh
closed	**chiuso**	kee-oo-zoh
left	**a sinistra**	ah see-**nee**-strah
right	**a destra**	ah **dess**-trah
early	**presto**	**press**-toh
late	**tardi**	**tar**-dee
entrance	**entrata**	en-**trah**-tah
exit	**uscita**	oo-**shee**-ta
toilet	**il gabinetto**	eel gah-bee-**net**-toh
free, unoccupied	**libero**	**lee**-bair-oh
free, no charge	**gratuito**	grah-**too**-ee-toh